THE SHINING HANDS

OF MY PONCA ANCESTORS

Contemporary Voices of Indigenous Peoples Series
Volume 4

THE SHINING HANDS

OF MY PONCA ANCESTORS

Cliff Taylor

NDSU NORTH DAKOTA STATE UNIVERSITY PRESS

Fargo, North Dakota

Dept. 2576, P.O. Box 6050
Fargo, ND, 58108-6050
www.ndsupress.org

The Shining Hands of My Ponca Ancestors
By Cliff Taylor

First Edition
First Printing

LCCN: on order from the Library of Congress at the time of publication.
ISBN: 978-1-946163-66-0

Cover and interior illustrations by www.wendyponca.com
Cover and interior design by Deb Tanner

The publication of *The Shining Hands of My Ponca Ancestors* is made possible by the generous support of the Muriel and Joseph Richardson Fund, donors to the NDSU Press Fund and the NDSU Press Endowed Fund, and other contributors to NDSU Press.

Kimberly Wallin, Director
Suzzanne Kelley, Publisher
Kyle Vanderburg, Assistant Acquisitions Editor
Emma Borah, Graduate Assistant in Publishing
Sara Quiring and Brandon R. Stariha, Publishing Interns

Book Team: Jamie Gilje, Katelyn S. Johnson, and Abigail CK Lill

Printed in the USA

Publisher's Cataloging-in-Publication
(Provided by Cassidy Cataloguing Services, Inc.)

Names: Taylor, Cliff (Clifford Cleveland), author.
Title: The shining hands of my Ponca ancestors / Cliff Taylor.
Description: First edition. | Fargo, North Dakota : North Dakota State University Press, [2025] | Series: Contemporary voices of indigenous peoples series ; v. 4.
Identifiers: ISBN: 9781946163660 (hardcover)
Subjects: LCSH: Taylor, Cliff (Cliff Cleveland) | Ponca Indians--Nebraska--Biography. | Spiritual healing. | Ponca Indians--History. | Ponca Indians--Rites and ceremonies | LCGFT: Autobiographies. | BISAC: BIOGRAPHY & AUTOBIOGRAPHY / Memoirs. | BIOGRAPHY & AUTOBIOGRAPHY / Native American. | LITERARY COLLECTIONS / Indigenous.
Classification: LCC: E99.P7 T39 2025 | DDC: 978.004/975--dc23

To Our Ponca People

May we carry the dreams forward
May we carry the culture forward
May we carry the spirituality forward
May we carry the language forward
May we carry these things—and more—forward
for the future generations
And may we live beautifully while doing so

It was noted that Standing Bear and other Ponca Chiefs spoke only the Ponca language during their lifetimes. This means that the primary language spoken well into the twentieth century was Ponca. In 1994 Louis Headman visited with Carolyn Knudsen in Niobrara, Nebraska. At the time Carolyn was one of the last remaining Northern Ponca who understood and spoke the language. She had requested a visit because she said she had not heard the language for many years. Many Ponca are expressing this sentiment today.

— Louis Headman (with Sean O' Neil),
Dictionary of the Ponca People

Grief expressed out loud, whether in or out of character, unchoreographed and honest, for someone we have lost, or a country or home we have lost, is in itself the greatest praise we could ever give them. Grief is praise, because it is the natural way love honors what it misses.

— Martín Prechtel,
The Smell of Rain on Dust: Grief and Praise

CONTENTS

WHAT BEING PONCA MEANS TO ME

ALMOST FORTY, I STAND AS still as a Nebraska Bigfoot and think about my life.

What does it mean to be Ponca?

There was a time, a long time, when I couldn't really answer that, at least not sufficiently. But now I feel like I can.

I was born in 1981 and came of age in a time of action figures, Arnold Schwarzenegger, and Nintendo. During that decade our tribe, the Ponca Tribe of Nebraska, was in a bit of a limbo, having been eliminated as a federally recognized tribe in 1966 with just 442 Ponca listed on the enrollment sheets. Where did we go when the government dissolved us as a federally recognized tribe? Nowhere. We continued living, growing, pushing forward with the story of our lives, struggling and rejoicing, skidding out and overcoming, being Indians and surviving no matter what.

In 1990, when I was nine and about to enter middle school in my hometown of Columbus, Nebraska, after much concerted effort and odds-defying work, our tribe was reinstated as a federally recognized tribe, with President George Bush Senior himself signing the Ponca Restoration Act. In my twenties, surfing the net on my night off, I remember coming across this newspaper article with my uncle Ronnie Picotte in it. When I asked him about this period when we'd lost our recognition, he said, "Other kids and other Indians in school would ask me, 'What kind of Indian are you?' and I would say, 'Ponca.' Then they would say, 'I never heard of that kind of Indian.' It would hurt when they said that. They were trying to get rid of us and it was like they were succeeding." (Try as I might, I couldn't find the article again to quote it directly, but this is how I remember it.)

In the '90s, I grew up and experienced a whole memoir's worth of stuff, getting into art, reading like a madman, negotiating the unspeakable realities of abuse, falling in love for the first couple of times, having real visions, and developing the character of myself that remains relatively unchanged to this day. I went to a few of our tribe's rebooted annual powwows, some funerals up in Niobrara, went back to Norfolk all the time to hang out with my grandpa and grandma and aunts and uncles, but didn't know much about myself as a Ponca, beyond the fact that I was one. I think this circumstance was and is the case for a lot of Ponca and other Indians today: we know we are one but that's about it. We're like a big garden bed in stasis, packed full of a million unique cultural and spiritual seeds, more underground than flowering, more potential than brilliant, ravishing ecosystem. Like an action figure still in the package, gathering dust in a drawer in the attic. That's how it was for me at least. I was a Ponca still waiting to come out of storage.

In the 2000s, freshly dropped-out of college so that I could go exploring and follow the material of all these visions I was continuing to have, I began to learn a little something about my Ponca self and identity. It wasn't easy, and yet I wouldn't have traded it for anything else. I was painfully insecure about how little I knew, even how to interact with other Indians, other Ponca outside of my family. I was shy like a freakshow oddity, tongue-tied, a shivering mouse. But in my heart, I wanted to know; I wanted to answer the questions that were racing inside of me. As fate would have it, at age twenty-one, I went to my first sweat. It was like I ducked into a portal and found myself immersed in a special eternity where my ancestral seeds could all rattle to life, my body could with great relief fill up with the essence of my People, and all my questions could become answers I never dreamed possible. At a sweat with Joe Bad Moccasin, the Indian doctor I first Sundanced with, he said, "My teacher, Joe

Eagle Elk, said that when you crawl into a sweat it should feel like coming home. That's how it feels when I come in here." That was how it felt for me too, I had come home. Home: the greatest thing I could hope to find as a Ponca, and now I carry it with me everywhere I go.

I spent my twenties gratefully traveling backward into my People's cosmos, Sundancing, visiting regularly and extensively with old people, consciously and unobtrusively filling a mental/spiritual filing cabinet with as many stories as possible, attending that annual powwow near-religiously and allowing myself to be saturated by it, connecting with and talking to my larger, extended family there. I attempted to wrap my head around as much of my tribe's contemporary being as I could, to follow developments via conversations, newspapers, events at my local Ponca center and elsewhere. I aspired to know the spiritual contours and dimensions of our tribe, stacking up all the medicine dreams I had, which cumulatively illuminated an undying infrastructure that held and carried the more visible landscape of our tribe's organism. I listened endlessly to everything my ordinary and inspiring relatives had to say, experiencing firsthand the healing beauty of how one can become a real, humble repository of their tribe's being and story.

In this way I found myself full of substance and soul, my inner life overflowing with the very things I'd felt myself tragically lacking and missing at the outset, my being now Ponca because I lived for my People and the work of seeing how I could be of help and service. Reflecting on it in this very moment, I feel like this was a miracle; a miracle the ancestors orchestrated not just for me but for many of us, so that we could embody what is truly possible for every Ponca and every Native who's out there. I believe this is what's waiting for everyone, when all our seeds get the right water, sunlight, and love; when all those millions of seeds get to crack open and blaze with life.

What does it mean to be Ponca then?

Being Ponca means going home to learn and discover that our culture isn't gone and in ruins but is actually an abundant, mountainous, living thing of beauty that's fully guided by the immense genius of our tribe's soul to this very day. There is more Ponca culture to learn than could ever be known and understood in a single or even several lifetimes; hearteningly, awesomely so. That's how it was way back when, and that's how it remains today.

Being Ponca means practicing our lifeways every day and watching with tears in my eyes how doing so shapes my life so that it begins to match the geometry, poetry, textures, feeling-spaces, and spirit of my beautiful, robust, potent, and deeply human Ponca ancestors. My face becoming theirs. My prayers becoming theirs. My story becoming theirs.

Being Ponca means being a passionate, forever student of everything that's going on with our tribe, of our history, traditions, cultural revitalization projects, language, customs, foods, and even of things that're kind of in the air/ether and not totally back in circulation yet. It means studying away with all my faculties, knowing that everything culturally and spiritually integrated into my person is added to the overall interconnected stream and soul of our People, including the ongoing lives of our ancestors and the coming lives of our future descendants. Growing the joy and healing within myself grows the joy and healing within my People as a whole, and I love it, fiercely and ferociously.

Being Ponca means living with my People's original ancestral homelands in my heart every day, that ancient root-system, that vibrant stronghold, that place where the Niobrara River pours into the Missouri River. All the memories I have of all the things I've experienced there in that cherished land swim about in me constantly, seasoning and flavoring me, tuning me up, keeping me thoroughly Ponca, guiding me like the voice of the land Herself.

Being Ponca means truly enjoying and embracing the dreams and responsibilities I've been given in this life, applying everything I have toward the helping of the People, in whatever concrete or mystical, direct or indirect, small or not-so-small form that may take. It means using my gifts and strengths to help my People and loving the grand design of however that all shakes out.

Being Ponca means following in the footsteps of my great-great-great grandpa Chief Standing Bear by trying to sniff out and intuit the ways that I can bring the humble and heroic values of his life into the matter and soul of my own.

Being Ponca means always remembering the gospel of what my grandpa Cliff Senior shared with me at the powwow one year when I was a teenager. It was dark and just the two of us were sitting at this picnic table by our tents. My grandpa was not a man of many words. Kind of out of nowhere, he broke the silence, saying, "You love your family no matter what. Whether they're an alcoholic or on drugs, you love them no matter what."

Being Ponca means always remembering my family and always loving them no matter what.

That is some, but not all, of what being Ponca means to me.

I love being Ponca, getting to carry my People's story through the strange land of this age, of these times.

I love talking about my People and sharing about our lives, about the spirit we live with.

I love that we are still here and that we have so much to say.

Almost forty, thinking about all of this, this Ponca is happy.

IF WE CAN'T POWWOW, THEN LET'S GO CAMPING!!!

WE BOUGHT OUR PLANE tickets. We crossed our fingers. We hoped against all hope. And then, as expected, the Ponca powwow was officially canceled.

"I get it," I said, looking at Aislinn on the couch beside me, both of us with our laptops in our laps. "It's risky. God forbid something bad happen. Everyone's gonna be bummed but they'll all understand too."

"It'll still be good to go back to Nebraska," she said.

I looked at her, feeling home just at the mention of it.

"You're right. It will."

We put our masks on and braved the travel situation, feeling not too afraid but also trying to be as conscientious and as considerate as possible. Mountains and clouds passed by outside the oval window; *Doctor Strange* played on the screen in front of me. When we landed my brother found us at the airport and loaded us up into his big truck.

"I'm in no rush," he said. "You guys want to grab a bite in Fremont?" Fremont was the halfway point between Omaha and Columbus.

"I'm starving," Aislinn said from the back. "Almost all the restaurants in the airport during our layover were closed."

"Dad said he wanted to go pick some sage up in Niobrara this weekend," I pitched in.

"How about we get some burritos?" my brother replied, Omaha roaring around us. "And I was thinking we could all go camping up there this weekend. What do you think?"

Aislinn and I looked at each other; we were thinking we'd have to rent a car for a day to get up there, but it seemed like maybe it was all just coming together.

"Cool," I replied. "That sounds great."

My brother stared ahead. "Burritos it is then."

Before we all piled into our pair of vehicles with our totes of gear, coolers, tents, and such, we all got to do what has become one of my favorite things in the past couple years since I left Nebraska: just hang out at my brother's with my niece and nephew, watching Netflix, walking over to play putt-putt golf, hitting up this one antique store in search of treasures, barbecuing, playing Unstable Unicorns, lounging, and just loving up on the little rascals and even my mellowing brother, too. Maybe when you're young you want adventure and encounters with real-life Native Jedi and to see the remnants of Atlantis, but then when you get older you just want to give your niece cool gifts that she'll remember you by long after you're gone and wrestle with your three-year-old mini-Godzilla nephew on the living room floor. Funny how the story changes as we get older, right? Funny and beautiful, too.

"Look out!" I yelled over to my brother, seeing my nephew's eyes widen and fill with fire. "He's beginning to transform! Here he comes!"

And then we were rolling up Highway 81 in a caravan of two: my brother, Aislinn, and me in one vehicle, and then his girlfriend and the two kids in the other vehicle. My dad was going to meet us up there.

We zipped through Norfolk, where my dad and his generation were from, took the old route through Pierce and Plainview, stories from the childhood parts of our memories splashing out, Grandpa and Grandma and relatives no longer around visiting us as we talked about and remembered them. "That market's where Grandpa always used to like to stop and get a whole bunch of meat," I told my brother. "Dad said he'd been going there since he was a kid."

It was a trip I'd been making since I was a little guy, always going back to Niobrara—where my grandpa and grandma and their generation were from—for funerals, powwow, visits, Sundance, and other things. The road back to the Ponca homelands. Always a little different every time we went back; always monumentally full of our People's soul. This would've been Aislinn's first time at our powwow; I really wanted to share it with her.

We hit Verdigre and continued beyond, the land becoming raw, wild, and original; no longer grids, cornfields, and flatness. This is where it got good. A familiar awe and love filled my consciousness. My eyes just kept looking and looking.

"Can you feel how it's different up here?" I kind of excitedly asked Aislinn, a geek to my core. "Can you feel all the stuff that's still alive up here?"

We wound up camping out in the smooth hills of Niobrara State Park. We'd decided on one spot and then after paying discovered a better, more spacious spot. "You all stay here," my brother said. "We'll go back to the office and see if we can switch over to this one." (My brother the following day: "The office was closed when we went back. We decided to not tell you guys and just stay anyway.")

We set up our tents down in this clearing that had a perfect shelter of treetops, felt the happiness of being away from TV and the city, felt the work/presence/history of our ancestors circling around the edges. We'd brought enough stuff to survive a week or two, but really we were just staying for two nights. The little guy ran wild. My niece double-checked to make sure we had the stuff for s'mores.

"Do you wanna go look at Niobrara from the shelter up that path?" I asked Aislinn.

"Yeah, let's check it out."

Up the path, there was a shelter on a hilltop overlooking Niobrara, the Missouri River, the bluffs, and South Dakota. It was maybe the best view I've encountered of the area, beating out my previous favorite of the high point at our cemetery even.

We stood on that open hilltop and looked at the whorls and breathing earth and beauty of everything. We were silent, happy. Neither one of us wanted to, or needed to, say a word.

That first night we made brats and a vegan burger for Aislinn and then s'mores; my dad finally showed up and he got himself all set up too, offering commentary on everything and anything, three coolers of drinks in tow, proud to be with his family.

When it got dark he went off to use the restroom and then told us when he got back, "I saw a falling star." He was gruff and sensitive, our resident Elder, a spoiler of the grandchildren.

"Do you want to go look at the stars from the shelter?" Aislinn asked.

She, my niece, and I walked back up the path returning already to the magic of that viewpoint. The skies were so clear, the stars infinitely visible, the Milky Way stretching and streaking through them all like an ancient celestial highway. We stood on the same spot we'd been to earlier, me telling my niece all sorts of things I thought it'd be good for her to hear.

And then we saw a falling star, big, bright, almost fuzzy.

"Did you know that when you see a falling star sometimes that's one of the little people coming down onto our planet?" I asked/told my niece.

And then we saw another falling star, slipping down through the brilliance of the other stars.

"Thank you for getting us to come stargazing, niece," I said. "All credit goes to you!"

My niece crunched up her face.

"You," I told her, "are the greatest Jedi of all!"

The next day Aislinn and I borrowed my brother's truck and went to our Sundance grounds in Santee. I had saved up two weeks' vacation and my tax return so we could make it to the Sundance this year, and then the global pandemic happened. At least we were going to get a quick visit in while we were up there, say hello, walk around, and touch hearts with the place.

When we got to the bridge near the grounds, we saw that it was out and under construction. We almost turned around until we saw that we were just supposed to drive down into the dry creek and go around it. It would've sucked if we'd come that far and then been denied access, you know? We were so happy to get there, though, and when we hopped out of the truck and saw it all, we could've done some sort of really sacred honoring dance and yahoo-ed our heads off and got to the teary part right away. I've danced eight years and plan to keep dancing more; many memories on those grounds, many more to come.

We hung out for a couple hours, fed a horse that was tied up there, checked out a huge new garden, blessed ourselves at the spring, left some offerings by the creek, prayed at the tree, sat around, noticed some new fallen trees, and sang some songs by where the sweats usually are. So much of our culture is about the upkeep and renewal of relationships, and nothing beats the in-person version of doing that when possible. I was very grateful to come to the grounds and feed my connection to the place, to the ceremony, and to my family there.

"If we'd come by ourselves, we would've camped here," I said to Aislinn, looking at the arbor.

"I have a feeling come next year we'll all be here together," she said, ever the optimist. "How does that sound?"

We got back and did a musical chairs thing with the vehicles, with my brother, his girlfriend, and the berserker nephew going to Santee to visit his grandparents on his mom's side, and my dad, Aislinn, my niece, and me going for a cruise over to the powwow grounds and the cemetery.

We drove along those roads that're engraved in so many of us Ponca, and my dad did most of the talking, sweeping back and forth between fond, distant memories, how much we needed to clean the coffee pan we'd borrowed and burned from Aunt Beverly, and a number of his takes on all the different things he had running around in his head. It was actually a warm, wholesome drive. A sign of how far we'd come as a family; how much we'd, believe it or not, healed.

We circled through the powwow grounds, waving at a bunch of relatives who were all sitting out by their campers—more folks who came to Niobrara even after the powwow had been canceled. We grinned at the new showers and restrooms, admired the cool work that was being done on the arena, took in the layers of life present, and peered at the statue of Chief Standing Bear standing tall a little way up in the distance. "I guess he looks pretty good up there," my dad said. "Don't he?"

Then, we went to the cemetery.

Since my early twenties I've come and walked our cemetery, putting tobacco on graves, praying, and singing. An immeasurably large chunk of our tribe's root-system is located there; I went to my first funeral there, my baby cousin Jacob's, when I was seven or eight. But this time we all followed my dad's lead, listened to him talk and recount family history, tell stories, tear up, describe important things that were not to be forgotten. At times you could feel the spirits pretty clearly; I paid especially close attention to what my dad got to talking about then. I really liked that my niece was getting to have this experience. She was being nourished in ways she might not understand now but that she would come to appreciate much, much later.

We stood by the fence, looking for the buffalo, all the graves behind us.

"Touch the fence," my dad told me.

"I don't know about that," I said.

My dad got a little misty, while also trying to hide it.

"Your grandpa was rough. That's what he'd tell me. He'd point at a fence like that and say, 'Touch that fence.'"

"All right then, here I go . . . !"

I did not touch the fence.

The second night, after s'mores and enough ghost stories to give more than just the kids the heebie-jeebies, I crashed out first, climbing into the tent feeling pretty bushed, and then a humongous, earth-shaking thunderstorm came.

"Get up!" Aislinn yelled, shaking my leg. "It's here! It's here!"

The one thing I miss the most about the weather and climate of Nebraska are the thunderstorms: cinematic, spine-tingling, pure reminders of the power of Mother Nature. But I was too dang tired to roll out of bed; Aislinn got to finally experience her first real Nebraska thunderstorm without me.

Everyone else stayed up and re-staked my dad's tent that had blown away, hurried some chairs and totes into this rudimentary shelter that was there, and just rode out the storm as it rumbled and struck and poured down upon the land. I kept waking up, listening to everyone, and smiling inside at the joy and fun I could hear in their voices.

"Was it better than the falling stars?" I asked Aislinn the next morning.

"Don't make me choose," she answered, sipping her coffee. "Don't make me choose."

We took off pretty early that Sunday morning, which would've been the last day of the powwow, because my brother's girlfriend, who actually worked at our tribe's casino, had a shift that night and needed to get some sleep. It was amazing how fast we broke camp and loaded things up. My dad said, "I'll meet you guys in Columbus. I gotta make a couple stops first, visit some friends." Somehow, he'd be cool to the very end, tough and unbreakable; the Ponca of his generation are still leading the way.

I was bit-up, red around my socks and waistline with chigger bites, and looking forward to a shower, air-conditioning, and downtime with the family in the living room. But before we left I wanted one last look. Everybody loaded up and I walked the short bit back over to the shelter and its view.

We Ponca are tasked with the blessing of trying to fathom the huge stretches of land and life we've inherited from our ancestors, that we've woken up into the vast, unending story of. It's like unearthing a million sacred artifacts that were buried in our souls by the ancestors right before we were born. So much, such a legacy, such a mysterious, generous, overflowing gift.

I looked at the land of Niobrara and tried to feel all the SACREDNESS that was there, in the rivers, the trees, the hills, the birds, the whole sweeping spread of everything.

I took it all in, felt mighty good and grateful, and then rejoined my family, everyone ready to get back to Columbus.

We spent a couple more days chilling with my brother, Dad, and family, and then we traveled back to Astoria, Oregon, where we've lived for the past year and a half. As far as I know, I am the only Ponca here.

The global pandemic has been a doozy, to say the least. So much canceled, so much chaos, so much time collectively spent in the dark of the unknown, so much tragic, actual death; hopefully things ease up as the rest of the year unfolds, hopefully everyone stays safe and finds abundant silver linings to all of the craziness. No powwow this year, no Sundance, but may we all still find those much-needed, much-sustaining experiences of precious togetherness.

"Next year you'll get to experience the powwow full-on!" I told Aislinn as we unpacked in our messy apartment. "I'll figure out a way to get you a vegetarian Indian taco and everything.

"Next year it's going to be on!"

SOME NOTES ON THE LITTLE PEOPLE

FOUR OF US SAT ON the sandy riverbank of the Skykomish River, a little fire going, our yummy food finished, empty plates stacked on top of each other. The conversation snaked and swirled, moved in congruence with the night, deepened, was rich. We started talking about spiritual things in Indian Country. I had a copy of my little people book, *The Memory of Souls*, with me and was already planning on sticking it under the windshield wiper of the truck of this other Native brother who was there, a poet who was camping out on the land and working on this cabin my friends were building. A good, curious feeling was in the air; you could feel that there were more than just four of us present.

"My auntie said that colonization is what made us afraid of the little people and the Bigfoot," the poet said, his eyes squinting, manner soft, neck tattooed. "She said they made us afraid of them because they wanted to break our connection to them." His words caught me like an epiphany, unlocking and explaining so much.

Our blond-haired mutual friend spoke next, nodding and saying, "You're right. You're right."

Age twenty-three. Sitting on the porch with my older, long-time art friend, Scott, and he hands me a book called *My Life With the Spirits*. "Check this out," he says. "This guy is probably the most well-known ritual magician in America right now. And do you know where he grew up? Columbus, Nebraska. The same place as us! Isn't that crazy? Read the first part of the Columbus section."

I begin reading about how this man had an appetite for the supernatural from a young age, and then he goes into a story about him riding his bike on the dike along the Loup River, going as fast as he can, trying his damndest to induce an altered state of consciousness so that he can hopefully see one of the little people! Scott knows that these little people have been coming to me pretty seriously and profoundly for the last two years, ever since I began learning about my People's ways.

"So, the little people were around the river and Pawnee Park where we were all regularly seeking sanctuary during our own spiritually-charged and active youth in Columbus? And this guy even mentions it in his autobiography!" I exclaim, just at the romantic beginning of my journey of learning as much as I could about these mysterious little relatives. "That's insane! That's . . . beautiful!"

For some reason I feel like Frankenstein in that one '70s Mexican art-house film, *The Spirit of the Beehive,* remembering that scene where his giant, patched-together self is hanging out with the little child by the lake in the yellow light. With my lanky arm I pull down this berry-laden branch for two little nieces at our Sundance, so that they can fill up their bowl for the aunties who're going to make us all some wojapi. We're down by the creek; the summer sun has us all cooking. "The last time we were down here we saw those little people," the older one says. "They were walking in the water—"

"Yeah! And we saw their clothes!" the younger one says, bright with her memory of these relatives who live in the woods across the creek at our Sundance. "They were made of leaves! Their shoes and hats and everything were made of leaves!"

Working with your spirit-helpers is revolutionary. The truth is we all have them: Indian, non-Indian, everyone on every continent everywhere. And our spirit-helpers are not concerned with only higher spiritual things. Generally speaking, we are a whole and they are concerned with all the dimensions of our lives. They guide us in heroic things, like the seemingly impossible undertakings we do for the sake of our culture's survival and transmission, and then they pitch in with other stuff, too, like making our uncle laugh, picking our partner up on time, or maybe learning how to become a better cook. The times we're in now especially need for us to pull out all the stuff we've got stored away in the backrooms of our spirituality—conscious, tended relationships with our spirit-helpers included. "Make an offering every day and see what happens," the little people once told me while I was out having a cigarette on my apartment steps in Seattle. Make an offering to your ancestors and your helpers, some tobacco or some of your dinner, and see what happens.

Feeling good about yourself in an honest sort of way can be something like a superpower. It's hard for a lot of Indians to feel good about themselves. This giant behemoth of a farmer—hard of hearing, far-seeing eyes—came into my grocery store once, and said, "When I was little, my mom, who was Cherokee, drove by some other Indians and said, 'Look at those dirty Indians. You don't want to be like them when you grow up.'" We Indians have been taught to hate ourselves and the poison of that runs deep; the government wanted us to leave everything on the side of the road and never look back, become an American, and pretend like we couldn't hear the constant crying of what happened to us, of what was taken from us. I remember walking to the gas station in the middle of the night in my twenties, feeling so utterly alone, praying and giving thanks to my helpers as I passed by an abandoned house. My connection to the little people burned bright in the dark as I prayed and my heart began to feel comforted, grateful, and good. Looking back and reflecting on how these little people have helped me, I can see all the ways they aided and empowered me to feel good about myself, to feel good about being Indian. Liking myself and not hating myself; what a superpower they bestowed on this Ponca, on me. I'll always appreciate that thing right there: the way they rescued me from my self-hate and taught me to feel good about myself.

A partial list of things the little people are all about: anything and everything with any artistry involved; poetry; deep storytelling and comedic storytelling; learning to sing old songs; GARDENS; learning about and developing relationships with plants and flowers; honoring mountains; distance healing and distance honoring (if you're unfamiliar with the latter, ask an Indian); the Sundance; Indigenous ways and the vital wisdom in their DNA, practice, and embodiment; paying attention to the nightly medicine of your dreams; not only respecting Elders but actively spending time with them; devotionally relating to Mother Earth; MUSIC; things made with love and your hands; community-building; becoming a human being who knows how to properly grieve; birds; the never-ending work of healing in all of its forms; PLAYING AROUND; tending and feeding that which needs tending and feeding; remembering ancient things with your spiritual organs that can do so; reinventing shit; real magic that changes lives and becomes an unbelievable story; an inspired human imagination; *The Lord of the Rings*; the bees and honey; and calling them when they tell you to give them a ring sometime.

It's a picture of love to me. I had this beautifully carved, small wooden statue of a cross-legged gnome sitting on my bookcase and, before I would sit down to work on my book about the little people, I would go up to this gnome and pray, peering into him like he was a portal into all of the smiling little people who'd been helping us Ponca since our tribe first came to be. A subtle feeling of sweet, heavenly joy would pass into me and then, almost inevitably, my third eye would begin to buzz; I'd finish praying and then I'd go over to my beat-up blue recliner and sit down, pick up my yellow legal pad, drift off for a second, and then start writing. All the spirits I wanted to have in my life were with me, the whole cast of characters I yearned to have by my side, crowding into the living room and the present. I scribbled away in my trance. No one in the world knew what I was working on, and I couldn't have been any happier.

When I was done with my little people book, I turned it into a zine: cutting and pasting it together at the university library, photocopying all the pages, and then folding them all together to make twelve bulky, finished copies. I gave all those away and then a poet-activist friend of mine used her hip Portland book-making skills to create 185 much nicer, semi-professional copies that could legitimately be called real indie books. I gave those copies away over the next couple years, discovering along the way a whole world of people who knew about or also had experiences with the little people. I randomly gave a copy to a Seattle cartoonist, and a year later received a long message from her detailing the experiences her younger brother had with the little people when he was a kid. I chowed down outside of the cookshack in Standing Rock when we were all facing off with the Black Snake, and listened to a woman talk to me about the little people parachuting down from the ceiling into her and her brother's bunkbeds, hearing how her mother told her not to talk about them, and then about how much medicine returned to her life when she finally started not just talking *about* them, but *to* them again when she was an adult.

The book was a force of pure magic and healing; a medicine book restoring spiritual connections of all kinds—lightning in a tiny paperback. I wondered where the book would go once it got out into the lives of the greater public. I wondered what those little people had planned for that book in all their strongest prayers and best dreams. I gifted away all my books and lived in wonder.

I meditated in my girlfriend's childhood bedroom, the house abuzz with conversation about what we were going to do now that our car was dead and our cross-country move from New Orleans to Oregon had ground to an unexpected halt. I relaxed deeper and deeper into the silence and stillness, communing with the Creator, and then, in the shut-eyed visionary darkness, I saw a little old man's wrinkled face and he began talking to me. "Don't worry!" he said. "You've got the luck of the Irish on your side. What do you think the luck of the Irish is? *We're* the luck of the Irish!" Suddenly, I saw all these scenes and instances where these leprechauns were doing all sorts of magical things for people, but then because these people couldn't see the leprechauns or didn't know about or believe in them, they just felt like they were getting lucky, *super* freaking lucky. "Don't worry!" the little leprechaun told me, and then he vanished. One month later, after truckloads of family bonding, healing, boardgames, and hangs by the fire, we were back on the road on our way to Oregon. That last week before we left, my girlfriend's dad put on his gear and treated us to a couple songs on his bagpipes; the music was so full of feeling, of memory, of meaning. *That leprechaun is probably with him*, I thought, *because he's carrying on with that traditional ancestral music*. I listened to him play, held my girlfriend's hand, and closed my eyes. The music was just so beautiful.

WHEN THUNDER MET LIGHTNING: THE STORY OF HOW I MET MY BROTHER DENNY

MY BROTHER DENNY was running on the treadmill that he'd somehow fit inside of his crowded kitchen, his big feet pounding on the track, intermittently speaking Lakota into his phone to reply to one of his language students on WhatsApp. Nona, my niece, fourteen years old and all glasses and dimples and long black hair that went down past her waist just like her dad's, was on the futon, splitting her attention between yet another episode of her favorite show, *Law & Order: Special Victims Unit (SVU)*, and the latest YA fantasy book she was tearing through. I was just waking up, a novel tucked beside me, fresh out of the shower with sloppy wet hair. I used to go visit Denny and the kids down in Lawrence, Kansas, for years when he was teaching at Haskell, but he'd moved back home to Standing Rock, and now I drove ten hours from Lincoln to come and visit them there. Our friendship was worth the drive. I would've piloted my rusty beast an even greater distance if I'd had to.

When Nona was little, she really took a positive shine to me: her dad's best friend, another total book-nerd, the brown-haired Ponca who was maybe a little softer, a bit more sensitive, a bit stranger than a lot of the other Natives who came around. It was cool to see how much she drank up all the goofball things I tossed her way; I always tried to make her and her brother, Pana, laugh, give them the kind of attention my largest-hearted uncles gave me growing up. But now she was on the verge of becoming a full-fledged teenager and all sorts of new elements were emerging from her person, like her obsession with *SVU* and Olivia Benson's never-ending search for perps and justice in the gritty streets of

New York City. Nowadays, I had to work a little more, a little harder to be the cool uncle. Sitting there, I think I was feeling a little experimental. And to be honest, I think I was feeling a few other relatives who were in the room as well.

Most wouldn't believe it, but I've probably had somewhere around four hundred or so dreams with my brother Denny in them over the years. We've just been in each other's lives like that since we first met, if you know what I mean. I don't have anyone else in my life that I've spent that kind of time with in the dreamworld. For years, I used to tell him that he should take all those hundreds of dreams that I'd texted/emailed/told him about and fashion them into a one-of-a-kind medicine-dream book to give to Nona and Pana when they graduated high school and hit that scary trail of initial adulthood.

"Don't you think they'd love to have a hundred pages of you and me adventuring around in the spirit world," I'd ask him, "learning from your grandpa and the spirits, digging on the gifts we're given, the things we're shown, the pathways that're described for us?" He'd always just shake his head and laugh, affirming that it was a pretty rad idea, but then taking no further steps to actually do anything with the big stack of dreams. Still, I've got my fingers crossed that he'll do something with them someday, pass them on and let those kiddos have them.

One thing we are both sure about though is that we're here to spend our lives not only making things better for the kids and the future generations, but also to set things up so that when it comes time to enact the specifics of their dreams and destinies everything will properly be in place. We both live this mission and are as casual about it as we are dead serious. With that in mind, we share lots of stories around the kids so that they can soak them up, absorb them, and file them away for future use. It's something we kind of have fun with, like a long-running series of inside family jokes. We've been there so we know how it's going to go. And it was in this spirit that I looked over at Nona, her dad still jogging away in the kitchen, and asked her, "Did your dad ever tell you the story of how we met?"

"No," she said, perking up.

I could tell that I'd caught her interest. Like both her dad and me, she could always smell a good story.

I decided to start off a little cornball and said, "Well, I think it's about time you learn that piece of our origin story. Like all good superheroes, we got one too. It's good to hear about how the spirits make people."

She shook her head and smiled, like my yarn had sort of a strange vibe to it but she was in. "My dad might be a superhero, but I don't know about you."

"Ouch!"

She laughed, putting Olivia Benson on mute, getting comfortable on her futon.

"Okay, I'm only going to tell you this story once," I said, "so you better remember it. I think it's one of the most important ones that I got . . ."

I was twenty-four years old, living in a small downtown apartment a couple blocks away from the university in Lincoln. I worked overnights stocking shelves at a grocery store with a bunch of self-proclaimed roughnecks, was writing a lot of short stories, and was about two years into learning about and walking the Red Road, with all the utterly powerful and life-changing experiences that entailed. I wasn't lost and without community anymore or clueless about my direction in life; now I was under the wing of our Indian Peoples, dedicated to Tunkasila and the People.

I had my first year of Sundance behind me and sweat almost weekly, but I was still sadly and painstakingly submerged in the work of pulling out all the thousands of poisonous trauma and grief thorns that porcupined me, working on my anger, wishing that I wasn't so lonely and looking for love. I rambled and stumbled around. I danced through whole CDs of music in my apartment by myself. I read a lot of books, watched a lot of movies, found ways to occupy my time, and had my routines. One of those routines was to walk over to the college union and check out all the bulletin boards to see if there were any fliers up for interesting cultural or art-related events that I wanted to go to, like a Native giving a lecture on something or some Tibetans creating a sand mandala. This was before Facebook, my analog way of catching wind of what was happening in our cool college town. I did it more than I needed to, but that's how I was back then: keeping myself together through rituals and routines, doing the same things over and over again, trying like hell to shake off my trauma and not succumb to it. A big portion of me was in survival-mode, hanging on by the skin of my teeth, holding on however I could.

One night I wandered over to the union and lonesomely made my way through the cozy halls, seeing all the bright college kids studying and laughing while I scanned the various packed bulletin boards, looking for the kind of thing I was perpetually hungry for but finding nothing. I went outside to the back of the union, lost myself in the big lit-up fountain with its boulders and geysers, and then went back inside, retracing my steps toward the front to make my exit, to continue my night wandering, my business of keeping myself company. I walked past all the same college kids and then, going through the first set of doors and catching it like a cup of cold coffee in the face, I saw this other Indian just standing there. He was well dressed, in slacks and an academic soldier's long, black coat, with two thin black braids hanging as still as unarticulated thoughts down past his butt. I was six-two, and he stood a few inches taller than me. My spirit read him in a flash: he wasn't really looking at the bulletin board in front of him, he was doing something that made sense in his environment, a sensitive outsider expertly blending in, figuring out his next move from a hidden vastness within himself. I read him very clearly and never stopped walking, so goddamned nervous in my own skin when it came to other Indians, who all seemed so much more real than me. I pushed open the door, releasing myself back into the night, leaving that other twenty-something Indian peer safely behind me.

The moment I began descending the stone steps outside, I started feeling all these sick butterflies in my stomach, feeling terrible because I'd caved to this sort of fear so many times in my life; in fact, I'd actually fled down these same steps about two years before because of an almost identical situation, which I suddenly found myself remembering with total shame and embarrassment.

Putting the union behind me, I remembered the time I'd seen this other tall, short-haired, obviously new Native kid literally standing still in the middle of the union's main artery, looking achingly lost with all the other college kids coursing around him. I saw him and thought of how many other Native kids didn't finish college because of there being no support system for them, because of how hard it was to be so far away from home, because of so many tough reasons really; how they'd dropped out, vanished, weren't able to see that potentially very positive and life-changing experience through. I also thought of myself, how isolated and alone I felt while I was going to college on that very campus, how I'd dropped out and left, how I'd never made a single real friend in the whole year and a half that I was there. I knew that I should introduce myself and go say hey, but I was just too paralyzed by the horde of fears that had had me in their grip since all the horrors of my indescribably abusive childhood. I wanted to reach out to this brother and dissolve the aloneness I saw enveloping him but, like what was happening now, I just kept walking, too fucking afraid to go and talk to this other Indian. And then I never saw this young Native kid around ever again, meaning he probably did wash out, go home, ditch college and embark on a different path. This haunted me as I walked away, my failure to reach out and give some simple kindness, warmth, and welcome to another Native who'd found himself in the city that I was beginning to love, where I'd eventually found so much joy, healing, and community. I'd dropped that sacred buffalo-hide ball once and now here I was doing it again.

I crossed the street and headed toward Wendy's and the two-dollar theater, feeling my fears and shame over how I hadn't been able to stop and talk to that other brother those years previous. The further and further I got from the union, the more and more those rioting butterflies ratcheted up their activity in my guts. But I couldn't help myself.

I walked without any change in my pace, long practiced at maintaining myself even as I experienced whole worlds within. I was on fire with my conscious failure. Then, about a block away, I heard a spirit say, *If you don't go back and talk to him, you're going to regret it for the rest of your life.* I heard the spirit clearly but kept on walking.

I walked and thought about it. The spirit said that I would "regret it for the rest of my life." What did it mean to regret something for the rest of your life? I felt into it, felt with clarity how at that point in my life I didn't have any regrets of that size or magnitude, and then I tried to imagine what it'd be like to have a regret like that, something that I carried with me to my dying day, a bleeding, iron-heavy thing incessantly crying in the background, irresolvable and of my own making. I traveled into what I'd heard and then, feeling how I didn't have any of those lifelong regrets just yet and didn't want to willingly incur one that night, I stopped and turned around, fixed my eyes on the union up the street, and began walking back.

There had been so many times in my life where the moment came to say the thing, to a girl I had feelings for, to my dad who was about to lay into me again, to a friend who was leaving for a good long while who I hadn't said goodbye to yet, and this smothering fear would steal my tongue and I'd watch my chance to speak come and go, and then I'd be socked yet again by that moment of what could've been just trailing away from me, not to be mine, not to be had. This very fear was aggressively thickening and crawling all over me as I walked back to the union, biting at me and trying to break me as my stomach butterflies all but burst from me, as I grew even more determined to make right on my last fuck-up, as I zeroed in on getting back to that bulletin board while not even knowing if that tall Indian brother was still there. I cut across the street, went up the steps, got to the door I'd exited from, and saw him standing there, still quasi-looking at the bulletin board. Not stopping for a second, I opened the door and went in.

"Hey," I said, standing behind him. He turned around, thoughtful and distant. He looked full-blood, slightly sad, had quite a bit of acne, and was about my age. A silence I recognized from my own inner being permeated him.

"Hey," he replied, friendly enough, slowly returning from his hidden depths.

"Are you Indian?" I asked, direct, not smooth, going straight for the room some part of me knew that we were both already standing in.

"I'm Lakota," he said.

"I'm Ponca."

"Cool."

We shook hands.

"I'm Cliff."

"My name's Denny."

"Are you new here?"

"I just moved here. For grad school."

"What're you studying?"

"Astronomy."

He made me think of a dusty old book you'd occasionally mysteriously come across at the library or in the laundromat, and sometimes you'd open it up and it'd just be blank or in a language you didn't understand, but then other times it'd be dense and alive and just packed with some of the most unique, original, and potent material you'd ever encountered in your entire dreamy, searching-filled life.

"What're you up to now?" I asked him, our connection pretty easy, both of us dialing into each other's energies.

"There's a dinner happening soon at the Culture Center. I was thinking of going to that." He looked outside. "You wanna go sit outside?"

We went outside and sat on the steps, the famously phallic Capitol looming over us, downtown Lincoln buzzing with life in the crisp fall night. Slowly, we got to talking, building out and painting our worlds, populating the scene around us with the giant-size contents of our interiors: comic books, chanupas, trailer parks, reservations, art, music, running, little people, old Medicine Men; we moved effortlessly from topic to person to experience as whole chunks of time kept falling behind us, both of us thoroughly and completely knowing that we were going to be spirit-brothers right then and there. We felt sacred, monumental things rising around us but kept it cool, each of us schooled in knowing how to conduct ourselves when the spirits were afoot, doing their lightning-charged work. We phased back to an age before the pipe was given to us, took in the air there, saw how different our bodies and everything else was in that time; we sprinted through booze-cratered, poverty-sculpted childhoods with our arms talismanically full of Stephen King books and things our grandpas told us; we were sun twins from different Nations pounded and hammered into a certain kind of unique, luminous shape and everything whispered about how neither of us had ever met another exactly like us before. He followed me into all of the different territories of my life and past, never taking a step back, always naturally relating to what I was sharing, and then he expanded our multidimensional conversation by realms with all of the shelves and shelves of stories he had from the reservation he grew up on and his family's ceremony history, all of which he rendered in a level of lucid detail unlike anything I'd ever experienced from another Indian. He was versatile, a peerless academic and intellectual, and then an even more gifted traditional knowledge-keeper; everything he said was fascinating, riveting, his stories completely mind-altering. It was like we were both drinking up a pure, healing light as we talked and listened. We were in the pocket of something long sought and wanted to stay with it. And I have no doubt that far above us in the starry heavens our ancestors were all looking down and smiling big at us as we both had finally made it to this beautiful, fated moment in our brothers' story.

After a couple hours on the steps, we left our spot and walked back to my apartment to grab my car. From there we cruised around just to cruise around and continue our epic conversation, firing at lightspeed, laughing and joking, asking whatever deep questions came to mind, following the stories that were pouring into the car, dumping out our dream lives like a pair of sacred nerds sorting through their wicked record collections. We speculated on the nature and capacities of various entities like serious students of Indigenous medicine, plunged into the truly legendary and holy life of his grandpa Sammy who'd had a long career as a powerful Indian doctor, tried to make sense of the cosmic paranormal strangeness that surrounded my art friends and I as we all shot through our mythological teenage years in nowhere Nebraska, and on and on and on. My car bubbled over with magnificent and comical memories everywhere we went. At one point we basically kicked down the door and barged in on the salty Lakota woman who was my friend and mentor, getting into a deliciously entangled, fireworks-and-laughter-filled, no-hold-barred spiritual conversation with her and her husband for a few hours, the four of us roaring with delight and a joyous hunger.

We drove across town to Walmart and wandered around in there like a pair of gentlemen Indian artists looking for somewhere to stroll long after midnight, browsing the DVDs, haunting the place, carrying on with our timeless explorations of Indian reality, ceremony, tribal history, the puzzles of our personal pasts, and the grand spirituality that guided all things. We zipped over to IHOP and grubbed down on plates of greasy food, drinking coffee, riding our conversation's expression of our People's boundlessness, caught up in the most magical all-night buffalo-blessed stone-witnessed grandpa-powered grandma-fed friend-making experience ever. We roamed, talked, incarnated an entire Indigenous universe, and just happily kept on going.

We talked and hung out for about eleven hours straight and then the sun began to come up and we decided to call it. He gave me directions to the professor's house where he was staying, and I dropped him off there. By then we were actually getting tired, everything feeling cool, easygoing, psychedelic and second nature.

"Give me a call when you're free for some more chatting," I said, roasted and spent, my Sundancer's heart glowing.

"All right," he said. "Later, brother."

"Later."

He walked up to the professor's house, and I drove off. It'd be years before I ever told him the story of why I'd turned around and gone back to talk to him, of what that spirit had told me. Thank Tunkasila for such guidance. Thank the spirits for such instructions.

And that's the story of how I met my brother Denny.

It felt significant to finally share that story with Nona, *SVU* silently on the flatscreen, her dad still running hard on the treadmill in the kitchen. For a moment, I saw myself as some ancient clown who'd volunteered to wear an entire planet's worth of feelings on my unshaven face; if it helped the young ones, then I was in. And now the story was hers. The capsule and seed of it, what it might become, was hers. With her it'd grow into something that it never could with me. Maybe she'd pass it on, doctor a friend with it one night in a truck-stop diner, patch someone up with it in the desert, help a skin to believe in our ways again.

"And then your dad moved into the basement apartment directly below mine and we really started hanging out," I continued, laughing some, remembering those five months he lived below me before he went back to Kansas to be with the kids. "It was crazy. I'd have a dream, wake up all wild-eyed, and then pound down on my living room floor, which was your dad's ceiling, and then if he was home he'd pound back up at me, and I'd go down and tell him all about my dream, about what the spirits told me and everything. He ever tell you about that?"

She shook her head, her mood shifting as I began to get a little everyday jokey again, the story she was meant to really catch and hear receding back into the safekeeping of now both of our memories.

"I remember you always coming to visit us down in Lawrence," she said. "That one time we got you to run on the track with us. That was funny. You looked like a drunk bear."

We both laughed. "I think I might've been a drunk bear in my past life," I said.

She shook her head and picked up the remote, un-muted Olivia Benson and Ice-T. In a couple years she'd send me a text telling me that she'd gotten accepted into the college that was at the top of her list. When I'd ask her what her major was going to be, she'd text me back, "Creative Writing."

Full of love in Oregon, I'd reply, "That's what I was going to guess."

I heard the treadmill power down and then Denny was standing there with us, taking in the *SVU*.

"You know who I think did it?" I asked him.

"Who?" he asked.

"The Indians," I said. "The Indians are always at the center of it all."

BURNT DOGS, OR, THE SUNDANCER'S FEET

THIS YEAR, FOR REASONS fairly obvious (Covid continues), we didn't have a Sundance. But I was thinking, in order to honor all the things that aren't going to happen at our ceremony this year, I would share a story about something that did happen at our ceremony many, many years ago. Somehow, that feels like a good idea to me.

For years now I've been intending to write a memoir about how I stumbled/was yanked into my People's ways, how I began Sundancing, rolled with Medicine Men, had visions, and discovered the Red Road. In fact, I've saved a small mountain of stories specifically for that book, but this story, the one I'm going to tell here, isn't a part of that mountain. I kind of feel like this story has been off wandering around down by a creek in Niobrara, nearly forgotten, spending its days rapping and singing to the woodpeckers and blue jays, all sparkling and silly. Just in case it never makes it onto the VIP bus of any other book, this is the story I want to give some life and time to today.

This isn't the place to explain all the twelve hundred moving parts of the Sundance, but for the story's sake I will say that there're basically four days of purification/preparation, and then there are four days of the ceremony itself, and this story begins with me on the third or fourth day of purification, during my third or fourth year of dancing. I was up at Hidden Valley, mute as a fallen leaf, still quite a way from overcoming all my fears and worries that I might somehow say the wrong thing and get booted from this holy center of the world which felt so much like my true home. I was grateful, worked at a gas station, had piercing scars on my chest. I was a Ponca healing up and on a mission to see our sacred culture revived and made as freely, potently, and as ubiquitously available to our People as it once was; I knew firsthand that our traditional ways healed our trauma and I wanted for my People to be healed, to be delivered from the colossal suffering that was crippling us and wiping so many of us out. I worked hard. I had dreams all the time. I was lonely. I was infinitely happy to be back at Hidden Valley, to be back at the Sundance again.

This particular summer we were really on top of things; getting the grass mowed, gathering up plenty of wood and stones for the sweat, prepping the spring that we were blessed to have on the grounds, and just doing good overall as a big family to the point where some nice little pockets of extended visiting and downtime were happening. I bopped around, listened to folks talk, laughed, stared up at the sky and watched the slowly-moving clouds. Somewhere in there, I found myself sitting on this riding lawnmower looking at the tree in the center of the arbor that we were going to have to dig out the next day, silently contemplating that warrior who'd been standing in the valley for the past year, dancing and doing things I could not imagine. Drifting on that mower like this, waiting for people to return from town so that we could get onto our next task, these three young kids came running up to me, all joy and aliveness and with a singular group question.

"Cliff! Cliff!" they asked, "Can you take us swimming? Just for an hour or two?"

They were all three the kids of our Sundance leaders, of the brothers who ran our dance. I was their uncle, a sort of half-alien from the city who didn't exactly talk like all of their relatives on the reservation. I was pretty uncomfortable in my own skin back then and hardly the first person to volunteer to take a carful of kids to our dance's preferred swimming spot fifteen miles away, but it was a hundred degrees out and there was nothing going on and then again who didn't want to see some happy kids made even happier, so I readjusted on the mower's hot seat and cracked open my fused-shut lips.

"Is it okay with your mom?" I asked.

"Yeah," the oldest boy answered, "she said we could ask you. We just can't stay gone all afternoon."

We all looked across to where the mom of two of them was sitting in her cheapo camping chair by their tents. Her smile was so essentially Indian and motherly that it should've been on a million posters everywhere. She waved at us, correctly assuming the content of our conversation, and gave us the thumbs up.

"Okay," I said, hopping off the mower, wiping the sweat from my forehead. "I guess we're going swimming. Let's roll."

(A note on my car: I drove a big old long Buick Roadmaster from the early nineties that had been my dad's slick drug dealer car when he'd been picked up and thrown into prison for a second time a couple years earlier. It had a deranged, smashed front end from when I'd hit a deer on the highway at 3 a.m., and then there was also a huge crater on the roof from when a streetlamp fell into it during a crazy thunderstorm. People cracked jokes about it everywhere I went but it got me around and got all sorts of friends and relatives who were always asking me for rides around too. "That thing's a tank," a mechanic once told me. "It'll never die." Making minimum-wage at the gas station and having no money for a new vehicle, I hoped he was right.)

More of a tenderfooted uncle than I knew, we all loaded up into my mangled Roadmaster and departed from the Sundance grounds. I turned on the radio, making sure to be extra safe and careful with these kids in my charge, bumped along the sketchy dirt road, hoping not to accidentally wind up in the gully that others had on muddier days, and tried to answer the different questions the kids had for me when they weren't busy entertaining themselves. The older boy sat up front with me while the younger boy and girl sat in back; perfectly behaved, wild, and golden-hearted. I always felt good seeing the kids at Sundance and dreamed of when I'd bring my own kids there someday, letting them take in all the love, old ceremony, customs, songs, spiritual happenings, and ineffable miracles that occurred there. In the book of my heart, I felt like every kid should grow up around the Sundance. It was just about the most beautiful thing I knew and what better experience to share with the children, especially in times like these. "Save the children!" my grandpa Zach would always bellow at the climatic ending to one of his favorite real-life stories he'd liked to tell. "Save the children!"

We backtracked our way along the gravel roads to the highway and then we joined the sparse traffic there, cruising under the blue sky, passing all the same ancient landmarks, their grandma's, the casino, the Pony, and then onward, hooking a right to the spot where we'd all shared so many unforgettable post-Sundance swims. There were a lot of young dancers back then, sons and daughters of the leaders, and the desire to go swimming right after the dance had ended mainly came from them. It was so ecstatic, so blissful, so beautiful and perfect. A caravan of Indians all freshly returned from the spirit-world of their four-day ceremony who hadn't showered in days, vibrant with otherworldly, ancestral energies, bonded, joyous, bloody, all running into the Missouri River, howling, laughing, teasing, tossing and sharing shampoo bottles, getting clean and having fun. It was easily one of the best life-moments I've been a part of in my forty years; even while it was happening, I was powerfully aware of its eternal beauty. No wonder these younger siblings wanted to go and hit up the swimming hole before we all potentially went there at the end of our eight days together. Why wait? Why not zip on over and plunge into those gorgeous waters now?

We rumbled down the final gravel road to our spot—the river running alongside us now—and, unbeckoned, I had this idea come to me, a sort of brilliant one, something that I was surprised wasn't already in circulation among us ever-wise Sundancers. Pondering the many hardships of the dance, my mind went to the scalding hot earth and how I could maybe proactively prepare my feet for the flesh-cooking ground out there in the center of our circle, how I could possibly get them ready somehow instead of just stepping out there with them all soft and sneaker-protected as they currently were. The positive energy of the idea whirled and ballooned inside my skull, sparking all the good parts of my reasoning faculties which I trusted. My first year, when I danced with Joe Bad up in Crow Creek, one of the leaders actually hooked me up with some duct tape to put on the bottoms of my feet, to help them with the scorching roughness of the arena, and I wore it until it fell off, whereupon my feet were then ready to finish the rest of the dance unassisted. And many danced wearing moccasins, which had to be helping them with the same issue, providing a shield and buffer from the razorblades of dried-out grass and that burning earth. I was a genius! Pulling in and turning off the car, I knew how I was going to do it: I would walk the gravel road we'd just driven down BAREFOOT while the kids swam and then that would totally toughen up my feet for the dance, making them more than ready for the terrain and all that we were going to be doing out there for those four long, timeless days. I smiled big. Good things always came from unplanned trips down to the river.

We all unloaded from the car and before I could explain my plan to go for a little walk, the kids were all three pulling off their shirts and shoes and running into the shallow river. They were all over ten and one of them was practically a teenager; they'd be cool. For a second, I felt a pang as I watched them splash into all that fun, imagining my alternate-universe self getting in there too, enjoying the water, carefree, still young too. I walked down and told them, "I'm gonna go for a walk. I won't go too far. Should be back in a little bit, okay?"

"All right, Uncle Cliff!" the older boy said, nodding, and then diving back under and out of sight.

I took off my shoes and socks and put them on the trunk of the Roadmaster. Immediately, I felt how seriously hot the gravel was. *Perfect*, I thought. Walking the road barefoot was totally going to transform my feet from soft and unworked to tough and ready for action. All my life I'd done things that others were afraid to do, that made others complain, that they wanted to avoid, or that was considered too much. I could totally walk on this sizzling gravel and endure some temporary pain and discomfort in order to engineer a smarter Sundance experience, no problem. I began walking. The trees were still, the brush semi-mowed, the boulders jagged, the river peaceful. I fell into my Zen, ignored the pain, felt kind of dreamy, walked closer and closer to my bright idea's successful execution. I heard the kids behind me and then I didn't. Like a poet-hearted automaton, I just kept on walking.

Growing up, my dad had a lot of different nicknames for me, including one of my favorites, Leatherback. Maybe after this, my relatives would call me Leatherfeet. I'd heard stories of Sundances that were far hotter than ours, that verged into the terrifying and unbelievable; things could always be even more challenging. The sharp, white gravel I was walking on had been baking in the upper ninety-degree heat for hours and hours by now. My walk became more and more uncomfortable the farther along I went. When I heard older Sundancers talk about what our ancestors went through so that we could have these ceremonies and still be living them and passing them on, I really felt it in the whole of my being. When the going got tough, you kept on going. And yet, as I kept on walking, my feet began to really hurt, and I began to wonder how much longer I was going to walk before I decided to call it and turn back. Then, considering all of this in the midst of my growing agony, I had a powerful realization: I was going to have to walk back the same whole distance that I'd gone so far, in effect, doubling the torment I'd committed to so far. I continued walking and then I stopped, feeling the full impact of my walk, my feet shotgun-blasting unbearable pain up into my sweaty, worried head.

Uh-oh!

My feet were seriously on fire and suddenly, desperately, I wanted to get back, get off the red-hot coals of the gravel road. Searching for any kind of relief, I hopped off the road into the bordering strip of brush but then jumped out of there even faster when my feet were both instantly pin-cushioned by a monstrous load of stickers. I clenched my teeth in anguish and methodically removed all the stickers from my feet with my two slobbery fingers, understanding that walking back on the brush was not an option. With nothing to do but walk the same road that had gotten me into my excruciating, foolish predicament, I semi-quickly began my return, comprehending my stupidity, feeling the screws twisting in deeper with each step, knowing it was only going to keep getting worse until it was behind me. I grimaced like a man being deformed by some science-fiction drug, like some crazed mutant who was about to go running off into the trees, like some Ponca flesh-ball of pure embarrassment and self-disgust. I was swearing and simultaneously trying to keep my wits about me, blaming no one but myself. I would've loved to have some grandmother spirit come down from the heavens to scoop me up and carry me back to my old Roadmaster, saving my ass from that snapping, mangling gravel, but there was no such grandma in sight. I looked ahead and kept on walking.

Eventually, I made it back and ran straight into the water, getting instant, merciful, total relief. "Did you have a good walk?" one of the younger ones asked me.

I smiled and nodded, giving no hint of the ordeal I'd inflicted on myself. "Yup. It was a good one."

I stood in the water and let myself buzz around that vast Missouri River space, listening to the kids, sensing the spirits of old Ponca, imagining them looking at me from atop the chalk-white bluffs on the South Dakota side. What had I done to myself? What a freaking idea. I definitely wasn't going to tell anyone back at the Sundance about my idiotic feet-scorching gravel walk; I didn't need that embarrassing story pinned to my ass and following me back every year for the rest of my life. I could've cried, but the private moments to do that had passed. I let the river doctor my feet and relaxed, wondering what in the hell I was thinking.

My feet were in pretty bad shape after that, the opposite of what I'd hoped for and envisioned, the opposite of how you'd want them to be for a ceremony where you're dancing from sunup to sundown for four days straight. They were extra tender, not extra tough. If I hadn't been so dead-set and serious when it came to the dance, I would've let myself limp—the pain was that bad. To my eyes, my feet looked burnt, with worrisome brown splotches on the heels and toes. It wasn't anywhere near as funny to me then as it is kind of now, where I have almost fifteen years of distance on the situation. Still new to the dance and afraid that I might not have the steel or guts to do what the spirits were asking me to do, I carried a genuine fear of not being able to complete the dance, of having to quit, to give up, which would've been the height of shame for my spiritually hungry self back then. Privately, I told myself that the only way I wouldn't finish the dance was if I died, like only death could stop me from seeing my sacred commitment through. I didn't have any blood-family to coach me or help me with these things, so I coached myself; getting myself to the next place the spirits had set up for me and then the next place after that. I was serious as a rawhide rattle materializing out thin air and then dropping down onto my stack of comic books. My fucked-up feet really had me worried.

We did all the beautiful things that we needed to for that year's Sundance: getting the tree, getting along, getting our pegs ready, making our crowns, bracelets, anklets, and then, skirted and properly attired, we began our dance. The morning sunlight on all our brown bodies. Ropes dangling from the tree. The train of buffalo skulls strung through with their big, frayed rope. There were about fourteen or fifteen of us, tightly knit, a seed in each of our hearts praying to the Creator, old dogs, young dogs, strict dudes, funny ones, bundle-keepers, gas station attendants.

I danced and felt good everywhere except for my cursed, burned-up feet. Every step I took banged some fresh pain into them. I kept it to myself, but I also could feel one of the younger leader's eyes on me; he was pretty gung ho and I could tell that he was reading my abnormally minimalist dancing-style as not gung ho enough. A couple rounds in, he said, "You know, we waited all year for this. We came here to dance. I want to see you all lifting your legs up. I want to see you all dancing." I might've been slightly paranoid and warped in the back of my head over this intense foot pain I was trying to secretly manage, but I took it kind of personally; but not personally enough to change my barely-lifting-my-feet dancing-style. I was all in with the rest of my being, but I wasn't going to push it with my feet. They hurt like I needed to go to the hospital. But I was willing to eat the criticism if it meant me making it to the end. I'd come to dance. I'd created this situation for myself. I was going to dance until we finished together no matter what. I prayed like I did every year; constantly, continually, every moving moment.

At the end of that first day, after sweating out and hanging up all my stuff on the nailheads under the arbor, after smoking a couple cigarettes and listening to the older brothers who laughed and joked and teased each other like they were literally the funniest Indians in the land, I curled up in my sleeping bag and checked in with myself. Spiritually, I felt good. It had been a solid first day. We were all doing what we were supposed to be doing and everyone was keeping a good attitude so far. A mysterious positivity was raining down from the stars onto all of us and we were all feeling thirsty but happy. But I was still worried about my feet. They weren't getting any better. I wondered if maybe I had some second-degree burns on them. A part of me was scared. So much rode on this for me. I knew from experience that the pains of ceremony could get worse, and uncontrollably so. Trust and prayer and fear flowed beneath my sun-cooked skin. I closed my eyes and fell into the depths of sleep.

Sometime in the middle of the night, with only the lone fireman sitting up by the fire, I woke up feeling kind of strange, half there and half somewhere else. Instinctively, I began to pray. One time up at Joe Bad's Sundance in Crow Creek, I was sitting with these two very unique twins who were both dressed in long black trench-coats and long black pants in the hundred-degree heat, when this other guy came over and started probing them with questions, sniffing around their spiritual gifts. This other guy wound up proposing a kind of test to these two WWF-reject-looking twins and then I listened as they told him that they'd consent to his test because they knew that their deceased grandma loved them so, so much that she'd come and surmount that test for them right then and there in front of everyone if she had to. Wearing just my trunks in my sleeping bag, I sort of felt the same as those twins. I believed that my two departed blood grandpas would come to help me in an absolutely miraculous way if I really needed them to, because they both loved me so, so much. This was a supernatural ace I had up my sleeve that I just KNEW was TRUE and REAL. And so, feeling scared about my feet, I started praying to them, my grandpa Cliff and my grandpa Zach. I sent my voice up to them, crying out to them wherever they were, praying for help, praying and praying and praying for their help. I expressed to them from the core of my soul how scared I was and talked to them both like they were sitting beside me right there, like they could hear my every word and were in complete possession of the means necessary to help me. Everything I was doing I was doing for my People, for my family and tribe. Cold and lying on my side, I kept praying until I was gone and asleep again.

An hour or so later, maybe less, I woke up again. I was aware of my surroundings but kept my eyes closed, was just a presence in my chubby body. I laid there and felt a big old sacred power, a big old sacred energy, moving and flowing around my feet, doctoring them; like dragons made of light closing their mouths over them; like huge swirls of spirit-energy emerging from the creek to engulf and heal them. I'd been around long enough to recognize the presence of the spirits. What was happening to me was completely focused on my feet, not working on any other parts of my physical body or emotional being; I was being delivered in an overwhelmingly real way from the painful part of things to the pain-free part of things. Waves and waves of indescribably soothing feelings rippled up into me from where the healing was happening. It was as tangible as the pegs that we put into our chests, as a coyote's howl in the night. I prayed and felt it all. I sensed primordial Taku-Skan-Skan there too. It must've lasted for maybe ten or fifteen minutes. Gigantic spirit-hands pumping the suffering out of me. Old powers fixing me up. Mercy being shown on my third year of dancing. I laid there, processing, and then I tumbled back to sleep.

The next morning, we all got up bright and early, just a little after 5 a.m., and when I swung my legs off of my cot and placed my feet on the ground, I felt nothing, nothing at all. No sparks of pain. No raw, cruel ouchiness. Nothing to make me wince, cringe, or dread being on my feet, let alone dancing on them all day. I looked at the grass-stained bottoms of them and they looked the same, still splotchy and burned, still not pretty (full disclosure: they've never been pretty). I slowly stood up and they were as good as they were before I'd dingbattedly embarked on my barefoot walk across that half mile of harsh, burning gravel. I walked over to the fire where there were a couple of others waking up and having their morning cigarettes. I felt that good feeling that comes when you're relatively deep into your fast and don't feel like shit but instead feel all those ancestors around you who are there to communicate their love, knowledge, and support. I blinked and stared at the fire. All the details etching themselves into my forever memories. Holy things to summon someday in the future when needed. I looked back at our pipes and saw our Sundance Chief coming over, round, dark brown, and smiling.

The rest of the dance was good. When I'd first Sundanced with Joe Bad he talked about how you couldn't record the dance in any way, no drawings, nothing. So, the largest part of the dance I will never write about; it's just not possible to; there're some places words just can't go, places where words kneel down and admit that they are meant to go no further. So many things happened. And I made it to the end. Classic Cliff:

sensitive orphan boy, Ponca who walked with the little people, young dreamer dreaming of all the lightning books he'd write someday. It was great. A bunch of the young guys all had their moms get them a van-load of food from the casino and then the moment they could, they smashed and devoured every burger, fry, chicken wing, slice of pizza, strip of bacon, and battered mushroom they could, every shining delicious bit; and then within minutes, they all ran over to the bushes and power-barfed it all right back up in front of everybody. I laughed, was in a cool Gatorade daze, couldn't believe what we'd all gone through, couldn't believe the beauty of the gift of what our ancestors and the Creator had given us. I chewed on my big dill pickle and had no doubt that I, as nobody special, had just experienced one of the greatest things that a human being could experience. Like that character in the Kafka novel *The Castle* I'd read as a teenager, I crossed my ankles and dissolved into everyone's bubbling pools of happiness and joy. The children running around. Talk of if we still had time to go for a swim yet or not. The cottonwoods creaking in the wind.

I go outside to the sweat that we have in our backyard, the place where I pray all these years later, where I remember things like this story I've shared here, and I just stand there. *What if everybody knew how to send their voice?* I hear a spirit say. *What if everybody knew how to pray like that?*

A PONCA WRITER'S DREAM

IN MY LATE TWENTIES, I had this dream: I was in one of these classrooms that was like a nice, clean trailer, like we had at my own elementary school when I was a kid; extra space for when the school itself ran out of room.

There were maybe seven or eight of us in there and then there was this Ponca Medicine Woman from the old times. It felt like a miracle to be seeing her, radiant with the essence of our People and tribe; undiluted, roaring like a waterfall, as big as the Plains Herself. We were all regular modern Indians. We were there to learn. She was teaching us.

She had this blanket or hide laid out on the carpeted floor and spread all across it were her sacred objects, ceremonial tools and instruments she used for her work. We all eyed them quietly; they were like a display that existed in no museum anywhere, that existed, as far as I knew, in no current Ponca household anywhere either. This was the window back in time I'd always daydreamed and fantasized about. I'd always just wanted to see what all of our stuff was like before America happened, before our removal down to Oklahoma and all the rest.

And now I was getting to stand directly in the presence of a true old Ponca.

The Ponca Medicine Woman, in a dress, her clothes telling a story I didn't have the literacy to read, pulled her hands out from behind her back and they were luminous, glowing bright; they had an aura, had visible sacred power moving and circulating through them. "In the old days," she said, smiling like a grandma happily imparting her wisdom to her grandchildren, "we would use our hands to heal just about anything."

Then, from out of the floor behind her, this arc or half-rainbow of seven boxes shot up, each one of them containing and illustrating one of the seven different medicines she worked with. There was something inside of each one but for whatever reason, I could only see what was in that first one, the one closest to the floor.

I took this all in and then, I remembered that I had to call our tribal chairman, Larry Wright Jr, for some reason I now cannot remember. There was a phone mounted on the far wall by the classroom's door; I walked over to it, picked it up, dialed his number, and waited, listening to the ring.

As I waited and listened, this deep and incredible sadness overcame me, possessed me like the greatest sorrow I could possibly feel. It was the utter sadness of failing to complete my life's purpose.

See, in the dream, as in real life, my twenty-something self had wanted to write some telephone book-thick tome for my Ponca People, a tome containing the near totality of our People's culture and spirituality, customs, beliefs, rites, history, stories of every kind, games, ceremonies, foods, EVERYTHING. I had wanted to write a big book with our whole Ponca cosmos in it that could travel to the bookshelf of every living Ponca tribal member and become a portal for them, through which they could learn as much as they desired to about our People's way of life, bring as much of it back into their own lives as they wanted. I aspired to learn everything I could and then write that immortal, game-changing book. All that was lost could never be lost again; not for us Ponca, at least.

But then I had failed.

In the dream, I had not succeeded in writing that fat, containing-everything, book.

And the terrible sadness I felt as the phone kept ringing was my feeling just how much I had failed, how much I didn't pull off my life's mission.

But then, staring off into the classroom, that old-time Ponca Medicine Woman and the other students standing at the other side, I had a true vision.

In the dream, I hadn't written that nine-hundred-page illuminated manuscript of the Ponca cosmos, but I had written this tiny little book, a slim volume, its spine probably no thicker than a few quarters. I didn't write the masterwork, but I *did* write a teeny, little book, barely a hundred pages; I did write that book.

And I felt so sorry because my tiny little book didn't measure up at all to the book I dreamed of writing, I had just fallen so short. What was my little book going to do? Nothing close to what that Ponca world-saving book would've, right?

And then I had this vision—

In the air before me, this map of Nebraska materialized, detailed, textured, full of rivers and counties and delineating lines. It floated and shimmered and then my tiny little book appeared in the vivid hologram of it, placed right by Niobrara, right in the middle of our ancestral Ponca homelands.

Holding the phone, I watched the vision come alive, animate, and I saw all these things, events, happenings, creations, ripple-effects, experiences, manifesting westward out of my book, visually branching and springing out of the body of my humble little book. Branches birthed branches birthed branches. All these infinite, uncountable things tree-ed out of my little book, growing wildly and beautifully across the hologram of Nebraska like super-powered spirited artwork vining out across a wall. I comprehended with my heart entirely what the vision was communicating to me and all my sorrow lifted, turning into the most beautiful human happiness.

The vision showed me, as I stood there, the million things that would happen because of the small book my imperfect writer's hand had crafted. I saw that the result was the same or tantamount to as if I had written that book my heart so long dreamed of writing; the impact of my little book would be the incalculable, immeasurable impact of a life's purpose utterly fulfilled, utterly.

I beheld the vision showing me the total, beautiful success of my life's work, felt the infinite soul-happiness that came with such a reality, and then I woke up.

I was doing what I'd done for years and years in Lincoln: reading and hanging out at the coffee shop. This particular coffee shop, The Mill, had this huge dock where you could sit outside and drink your coffee. It was just a couple blocks away from the university, across the street from the best Indian food restaurant in town; a great people-watching spot.

I was by myself, my feet up on the brick planters that lined the dock's edge, sipping my coffee, and reading my book. It was my day off. It was summertime and sunny out. I had no plans that day, was just paddling through it. Cliff the Ponca Poet enjoying his fifteenth year in Lincoln, Nebraska.

And then I heard a voice from the Mill's doorway behind me: "Hey, Cliff! Come in here for a second! There's someone I want you to meet!"

It was Amy, a redheaded, freckled photographer my age who'd recently gotten a job as the executive director of the John G. Neihardt Foundation. I smiled and waved and got up. I always felt like an entire planet that people only saw the shoes of back then. I liked Amy because I knew that she saw a little more of me than just my shoes.

I went into the coffee shop and Amy was standing in line with a very old Indian man, dressed in the kind of clothes a plain and respected Elder might wear to a college class he was invited to speak to. He was maybe in his late seventies, had glasses and was thinner, and looked a little out of place in the hipster's milieu of the coffee shop.

"This is Louis Headman," she said. "He's Ponca from Oklahoma. He's just passing through town. I'm so glad you're here!"

We shook hands and I told him who I was, who my family was, where we came from. He seemed happy even if he didn't immediately start gushing or opening up too fast. He began to tell me what he was in town for, and I listened respectfully, my spirit solemnly receiving the gifts that were coming from the planet of his person. Louis Headman. I'd heard of him before. We Northern Ponca were slowly widening relations with our Southern Ponca relatives in the work of cultural exchange and the rebuilding of our Nation; my understanding was that the Southern Ponca were substantially more intact, had held onto a lot more of our culture and lifeways than we did. I had heard Mr. Headman's name in conversations regarding such things.

"I'm working with a gentleman at the university here on a Ponca dictionary," he said. "It's almost done. It should be coming out sometime next spring or summer."

Amy, giving us some time, went forward with everyone else in the coffee line while we broke away.

I could feel something inside of me guiding my words; it's something that happens when I get to talk with one of these old ones who carry a lifetime's worth of the most precious knowledge. As a seeker and a Sundancer, I was a link in the chain of intergenerational cultural transmission, and as much as I loved comic books and horror movies and messing around, I knew it was my sacred responsibility to make things better for the generations that were coming after me. I spoke the question that came to me, which somehow cut to the heart of the matter.

"How many fluent speakers of the language are left?" We Northern Ponca had no fluent speakers of our Ponca language.

"There are three elderly women left who're fluent speakers," he answered, "but one of them refuses to speak to anyone."

He wasn't counting himself, which would've made four speakers left. For the briefest second, I let myself feel the full gravity of this reality, a fact I didn't know. Then, I asked him, "What does that mean for the fate of the language?"

"It's dead," he answered, catching me a bit off guard. "All we can do now is preserve it for people to study in the future, like people in college study ancient Greek. It's no longer alive, but it's not completely lost either. There's one young man back home who's completely immersing himself, but in a couple years there'll be no one left for him to talk with or be corrected by. The culture is embedded in every word of the language. The language is a whole complete library of the culture."[1]

I absorbed everything he said, and he continued on, talking positively about the fluidity and adaptability of the culture, about his time in the seminary, a tradition he once tried to reintroduce, and his dad, who was born in 1890. For my part, feeling uncharacteristically open, I told him, "The spirits have been talking to me about our People and about writing some books for a very long time . . ." and then I shared about my little people book, running outside even to grab a copy of it from my bag to gift him ("This is a very beautiful cover," he said. "Did you draw this?"). He was very approving and encouraging. When I'd given a printout of my book to Amy a few months earlier, she raved about it but then followed up with how she'd spoken to a Ponca Elder about the little people and was told they were a negative subject not to be brought up. Mr. Headman was kind, and when I spoke of the little people he communicated a respect in his manner that felt like an Elder from my own tribe sincerely wishing me the best of luck in my spiritual studies and goals, which was something that always felt pretty rare.

Our time was short, but one last memorable thing he shared was something his dad had told him when he was a young man, something that felt so on-point in the moment that I was hesitant to believe it, even though I knew that I was meant to. He was talking some of his dad, telling a few stories, and he said, "My dad said, 'You have this gift and people are going to think that there's something wrong with you because of it. But that doesn't matter. This gift is yours to help the People with, and it

[1] In the decade-plus since this conversation, our tribe has developed a robust and ever-growing Ponca language revitalization program. A relative in a dream: "Fluency can return."

doesn't matter if no one understands it.'" He then went on to say that his dad's statement had accurately described the long-term path of his life, all the way up to the work that he was doing today. I heard those words his dad must've said to him sometime in the 1950s and felt like the invisible unfolding of my own life's destiny had been spiritually seen. I felt like that ancestor born in 1890 was speaking to my young-self right then and there, too.

Amy came back with their two drinks, and it was time for them to go. I scribbled down my contact information and gave it to Mr. Headman, shook his hand one last time, and waved goodbye to them both.

I could've staggered out of that coffee shop back to my seat, but I'd spent a lifetime learning to keep my shit together and just walked back out to my lonesome post feeling blessed; kicked my feet back up and looked at all the different people passing by on the sidewalk.

At age thirty-four, I'd finally gotten to meet my first fluent speaker of the Ponca language, of my tribe's language. It was like there was some mythical tree with a trunk as wide as a building up in our homelands and even though at one time our People's village was perpetually centered around that trunk, we following it, it following us, nowadays most of us Ponca were lucky if we got to glimpse it even once in a lifetime. Meeting Mr. Headman, I felt like I got to spend about fifteen minutes straight with that tree, the winds of multiple eras breaking against us, me leaning on it, its essence pouring into me.

I picked my book back up and daydreamed about Ponca families in the far-off future, where every one of them had at least one Mr. Headman constantly nearby, if not two or three or four, just like in the old days.

Last year, a couple years later than planned, Mr. Headman (with Sean O' Neal) published the *Dictionary of the Ponca People* with the University of Nebraska Press. I paid my sixty-five bucks for the book of about five thousand Ponca words, and then I sat by my window in rainy Astoria waiting for my copy to arrive. The prayers and efforts of thousands upon thousands of ancestors condensed into about five thousand uncorrupted words, preserved in the modern stuff of paper and books. Their breath, vibration, echo, powerfully alive in every word. It was a monumental achievement. When it finally came, I unwrapped it and tried to fathom it, knowing I probably never would. How do you fathom something that by its design is not meant to ever be fully understood in the span of a single human lifetime? Only the heart knows the answer to that question.

And then I really had my Ponca soul rocked when I learned that Mr. Headman had a second companion book coming out a few months after the dictionary titled *Walks on the Ground: A Tribal History of the Ponca Nation*. Its description said that it clocked in at nearly six hundred pages. I paid ninety bucks for that one and then also waited, on this passionate cultural learning/healing journey for over twenty years without any such book just like that to read, study, and ponder. Far from home, almost forty, unimaginable Ponca books were coming into existence. Two gifts falling down from the heavens, made legible for us by the hands of an Elder. Who else out there was feeling this special, sacred joy?

A note on Northern Ponca books: until my memoir, *The Memory of Souls*, there were none. Meaning, until I'd published that book, no other Northern Ponca had ever published a book; there were no books written by any of our tribal members for us to read and get a knowledge or understanding-infusion from. One time at our powwow in Niobrara when I was about twenty, an auntie told me that her brother had written a small memoir about his being the first Indian bartender in Norfolk, Nebraska, but that it was never published and had been lost to the sands of time. That was the only Northern Ponca-authored book I'd ever heard of. Primarily, we've had one real substantial book on the shelves about our tribe: James Howard's *The Ponca Tribe*, which was originally published in 1965 as a bulletin by the Smithsonian Institution's Bureau of American Ethnology. It's a useful, essential text, but specialized and not for your average reader or Ponca. Books are such a powerful means for transmitting and circulating knowledge, stories, even consciousness and spirit. I highly doubt that I've been the only Ponca in the last hundred years who's lonesomely found themselves surrounded by mountains of books only to lament the painful fact that there wasn't a single one about our People written by one of our own. I doubt I've been the only one to contemplate that particular sadness as it was trailing behind us along with all of the rest.

But then, BAM! Through the beautiful, never-ending collaborative work of our fantastically present ancestors (which constitutes a real, indestructible part of human reality), things changed, longings were answered, and prayers transformed into world-altering events and objects, books even, Ponca books even!

When I finally received my hardback copy of *Walks on the Ground*, I felt like I had in my possession the book my twenty-something self had always imagined it was my impossible task to write: a gargantuan, informative, radiant book of Ponca culture and history that could serve as the quintessential Ponca-authored resource on our tribe. Although Mr. Headman is a Southern Ponca, his book emanates from such a deep place that it encompasses the history and evolutionary progression of both our Northern and Southern Ponca Nations (for the most part). In the introduction, he states that the book was assembled from notes, interviews, and testimonies that he had been actively gathering for nearly seventy years, reaching all the way back to those Ponca who were the last to come-of-age in Niobrara before our tribe's removal. It's a priceless text, a true life's work; way beyond anything I've been positioned to write for the tribe in my lifetime. When I pick it up and read it for a while, my spirit lifts up and the ancestors literally begin talking to me. These are the kinds of books Natives can write. This is why I wanted to have a book written by a Ponca for all those years; I knew that it would help me to HEAR my ancestors, and my heart yearned to HEAR THEM MORE. The book of my Ponca dreams is here, and I guess it was never mine to write. Thank you, Mr. Headman, again, for the life you have lived so that you could bring us these two invaluable, all-important books. Thank you.

Now, about that dream—

Last year, I officially published *The Memory of Souls*. To me, it's a prayer of healing for my People, especially our young People. I wrote it after the spirits wrote it for me, in front of me, in a pair of dreams, crafting it down to its finest details; after the dreams, they put it as a finished thing into my body, leaving it to me to write it in this world. I carried the manuscript of that book for a long time, and then when Covid hit I got serious about publishing it myself and getting it out there. Who can ever guess the way these things finally choose/come to happen?

Over the years, I've often wondered if *The Memory of Souls* wasn't the slim little volume my dream-self had written in my dream about my writer's destiny as a Ponca. In our artist's heart we aspire to have some deep, profound impact with our work, aiming to transform the very culture into something more soulful and sensitive, something more akin to the realms which are the source of our inspirations; and we often assume a certain size and heft is necessary to make that real, lasting impact, hence the massiveness of the tome my dream-self thought he had to write. But the spirits are not so linear, so simple, when it comes to weaving their influences into the organism of the culture; they can change a civilization's course with a single kiss, as much as we might think we need an atom bomb. They can use some gas station clerk's handwritten, hundred-page storytelling about how the little people took him on a healing journey that matched up with the soul-needs of his People and create a seismic medicine-outpouring into the land and consciousness of his Nation that's more subtle and permanently shifting than any manmade technologies currently have the capacity to measure. Right?

Like my mom always used to say when I was a kid, "Only time will tell."

I'm not sure what'll happen with my crazy little book, but I am glad that it's no longer just gathering dust in a moving box with the rest of my unpublished manuscripts; I am glad that it's now out there for my Sundancer's ideal heart-imagined audience to discover. I'm happy that after twenty years of seeing this empty Ponca bookshelf in my mind, there's now at least one title on that shelf written by a Northern Ponca, making it empty no more. I love to honor and feed the reality of how it takes just one person to do something for that something to then flare up and become a force of real dynamic change in the hands of an uncountable many. I hope my book helps our People to remember the immense dignity, beauty, wisdom, spiritual power, and imagination that we have inside of us as Ponca; and that in the remembering of this luminous ancestral cultural inheritance, we get a better grasp of what's available to us so that we can make a more beautiful life for ourselves and everyone around us. That's maybe the biggest part of the prayer my book is articulating in its hundred or so pages.

Is it the book that my vision in that dream was communicating to me about, showing me all the happenings and happiness that would come of it?

I don't know.

But like my mom said, time will tell.

I was twenty years old, driving the forty-five minutes it took me to get from Columbus to Norfolk. I had some spare time and wanted to visit the super kick-ass movies/music/comics/and books spot, Hastings Bookstore. I was at the beginning of my life and there were just so many brilliant and important books to discover. Back then, few things were as bright for me on the prairie as a cool bookstore.

It wasn't a long drive, but it felt like one at that age because I'd been driving for such a short time. I passed Madison, that one permanently shut down gas station I'd been seeing since I was a kid, Ta-Ha-Zouka Park where I'd gone fishing, the viaduct, and then I was there, Norfolk, the city where my dad grew up and where most of his family still lived. My mind was happy and open; my body rippled with how much I loved art, how much I yearned for a life like Kerouac wrote about in *On the Road*, how much I FELT the enormous force of life flowing through my soul. Then, completely non-sequitur, a thought entered my mind that I should go and visit my grandpa Zach, my mom's dad, who had recently been relocated to the veterans' home in Norfolk. He was eighty-two, a WWII Veteran. He was deaf in one ear, had about 10 percent hearing in the other ear, and was almost completely blind. A small book was written about the ship he served on and when he gave me a copy of it, his inscription read, "I loved her dearly." I felt the same way about him; I loved my grandpa dearly.

Following that thought like a clear directive, I cruised right on by the turn to Hastings Bookstore and continued on to the veterans' home, finding a parking spot and not thinking twice about how I'd never actually visited him by myself, how strange it was that I was so casually doing something that I'd never done before. I got out of my car, walked in, and went straight to the front desk.

"Hi. My name is Cliff Taylor. I've come to visit my grandpa, Zachariah Boughn."

The nurse was friendly, and she immediately looked him up. "Okay," she said, "He's just down the hall. I'll take you to him."

I followed the nurse, passing rooms with all sorts of elderly people, papery, white, lots of tubes, some of them sitting up, many lying down. The rooms were like little monk cells with flowers. Quiet, contemplative. Windows looked out at blue skies with big clouds in them, still and eternal.

"Here he is," the nurse said, leading me into my grandpa Zach's room. I looked at him and lovingly grasped his state right away.

"Zach! Zach!" the nurse yelled into his one partially working ear. "Your grandson is here to visit you! Your grandson! Cliff!"

My grandpa Zach laid on his back under a light sheet, nothing to occupy him but his thoughts and memories, his head shaved, eyes looking up, catheter snaking out the side of his bed. My grandpa, when he could no longer care for himself, moved to the old folks' home where my grandma Julia, who had severe Alzheimer's, had been for the past decade. A few years later, he had himself transferred to the veterans' home; he said that he wanted to be with others who had served when he died. He looked okay but this was his last stop. There was nowhere for him to go but up from here.

"Cliff!"

A light moved through him; a body-wide flash of pure happiness. I bent down to his ear.

"It's me, Grandpa! It's Cliff!"

"Oh, Grandson! How are you doing?" His hands started reaching up and searching for mine. I grabbed his hands and held them. The nurse brought me over a chair.

"I'm doing good, Grandpa! I came to go to the bookstore here in Norfolk!"

"The what?"

"The bookstore!"

"Oh! That's good! That's good!"

The nurse bent down beside us.

"If you need anything, just let us know, Zach!" She seemed genuinely nice.

My grandpa, unable to help himself, swelling with love and pride, said, "This is my grandson! My daughter Gina's boy! He's Native American! He's Ponca and Sioux! He's a good young man!"

"He looks like a good young man!" the nurse replied, and then she smiled and left.

My grandpa, German and Irish, a retired high school history teacher, always transmitted the most protective love, gave me Indian books that emphasized the Indian side of the story, and never made me feel anything but good about the Indian half of my being and my dad's People. It was awesome, like visions that can transform a person's entire understanding of themselves are awesome; like Indigenous Creation Stories and Nebraska thunderstorms and the Sundance are awesome. I still have every single book that he ever gave me.

My grandpa and I talked in this loud manner, him blind, me talking into his ear, and every moment had him sparking and rising with life. It was a joy. It wasn't long, probably forty-five minutes, but it was an unforgettable, indelible visit. Toward the end, he asked me something he'd never really asked me before. He asked me, "So, what do you want to do when you get older, Grandson?"

It was just one of those moments. I'd been a hider all my life, always hiding the things that were to me my true life. I'd been severely abused growing up and had learned to keep all the vulnerable realities of my soul a million miles away from anyone who could cause them even the tiniest bit of harm. Only my few closest art friends knew that I wanted to be a writer. But now I wanted my grandpa to know too; I wanted my soul's calling to be something that he knew too. I wanted my grandpa, lifelong lover of books, whose library of four thousand books had been donated to Wayne State College (the place where I spent the first five years of my life living in the dorms with my mom while she was getting her teaching degree) when his house had been sold, to know the purpose that was at the center of his grandson's life, to know why I was here.

"I want to be a writer when I grow up!" I bravely said. "I want to write books!"

"Oh!" my grandpa replied back, exhaling so much love into me from his being. "That is wonderful! A writer! We have not yet had a writer in our family!"

They were words of approval I would never forget. What a special blessing it is to have your soul seen by a grandparent whom you love with all your heart.

In speaking it aloud, I felt like I was making a promise. A promise not only to myself but to my grandpa, that I would become the thing I came here to be. I promised to fulfill my dream of becoming a writer.

We talked loudly, held hands, and then we said goodbye, hugging, and feeling the Spirit move between us as we did. I had no idea that that would be the last time I'd ever see him alive. I walked off, waved to the nurse at the front desk, got into my car, and went to the bookstore, spending hours among the shelves and shelves of glorious books. Bought myself one even. And then cruised on back home and carried on with my day.

Voices have spoken to me my whole life and I have listened to them; I am a result of listening to them. I sure am grateful for that voice that told me to go and visit my grandpa. That voice probably knew that that would be my last chance to see him, to hear his voice, to receive the blessings that he still had to impart to me; that voice surely knew how important such a last visit would be to me.

About ten years ago, on New Year's Eve, I had a dream with my grandpa Zach. We were in an empty movie theater, sitting beside each other in the back row. My grandma Julia was standing behind us. On the screen, the movie's opening titles began playing, a movie I'd never seen in real life: in thick red comic book letters it said *THE SPIRIT*.

My grandpa Zach came to me many times in dreams after he died. I loved seeing him. He had that power to reach me from the Other Side. But in this dream, we both knew that this was going to be the end of those dream visits, because their course had run complete. In this dream, he would pass his power on to me, the power he'd had since he was a little boy when he was alive, that all our family talked about.

We both started to cry and leaned in and hugged each other, held each other, sobbed. I could feel something leaving him, entering into me; an energy transferring over from him to me.

He was consoling me.

He was saying goodbye.

He was adding his gift to mine.

"That is wonderful! A writer! We have not yet had a writer in our family!"

I felt the last of what he had to share pass into me and then I woke up.

THE RAIN THAT WASN'T WET

I WAS ON THE VERGE of a major life-change but didn't know it yet. I had been in the same downtown apartment for fourteen years, had been working at my gas station for an entire delicious decade, had been tirelessly running the same routines from my teenage years through to my mid-thirties: read, write, pray, meditate, sweat, Sundance, repeat. There was this droplet of holy dew in the bottom plastic shirt button of my soul, and I was just hunched over trying to squeeze it out with both hands and all my might and my life was just quietly passing me by.

And now, here I was camping out in Niobrara with these two incredibly beautiful women who were on a cross-country tour spreading the word about the little people, doing ceremonies wherein people actually got to hear from these powerful little relatives. They were selling my little people books to folks along the way and sharing reports of just how many people of completely diverse cultural backgrounds had had experiences with these little relatives. It was a whole book's worth of stuff unto itself, for sure, but now the two of them, my new friends Sarah and Chelsea, were in Nebraska (which they'd inked into their tour just because of me) and I was very nervously and not too confidently showing them around (they were way more savvy, adept, gifted, and spiritually experienced than I'd expected, and I was basically a nameless dude who'd never left Nebraska). The first night we stayed in my apartment. The next night we drove three hours north and camped out at the Sundance grounds. This night we were at my tribe's powwow grounds. And tomorrow we planned to stay with my writer friend Barbara. Then it'd be back to Lincoln for me and the road for them, continuing on with the second half of their tour. My world was being electrified by their visit, by their threading into and through my life, and more so than I knew or had any idea about.

It was late. We had our tents where people usually put up their tents during the powwow and it was well past midnight. Sarah, always early to sleep and up before Chelsea and me, was already tucked away and crashed out in the nice, smaller-sized SUV they were traveling in. Chelsea and I were by the fire, feeding it, heading deeper into a new cavern of conversation that was a part of this whole epic world of conversations the three of us were having, that she and I were having. Things I'd talked about with only a few or with no one at all, were coming up and pouring out of me, all this shit in my soul untwisting, emerging, breathing, collapsing, asking to be witnessed. I'd been in my own world for so long, probably too long. It was so healing to share so much unshared stuff with these kindred spirits that this visit was almost surely the thing responsible for catalyzing my major upcoming and unforeseen life-change. Thank Tunkasila that we live in a realm where such crucial, unexpected, and profoundly healing things can really happen. The alternative would be impossible to bear.

Chelsea and I must've talked for maybe three more hours after Sarah went to sleep. She had sandy-blonde hair, a masters in anthropology, was an exquisite, articulate lover of Nature, knew a lot of the same esoteric spiritual realties as myself, and was just beautiful; the kind of woman my perpetually single-self could've crushed on for far, far too long. The night was thick with things that were completely particular to these lands, and the wonder and specialness of where we were at was not, and could never be, lost on me. I loved those hills, those stars, the saturating history, the nearby cemetery, the buffalo pasture behind us, and the Ponca landscape encircling us. And Chelsea got it. As I kept poetically drawing this and detailing that, she not only felt me but had all sorts of big and small ideas to add to the mix that were causing me to see so much that I felt I'd been carrying by myself differently, in a way that enlightened and unburdened me. I was getting something that I longed for and I just cried, let it out, laughed, kept going, seeing in her eyes something that I wished for all of my friends and enemies alike: true selfless love and understanding, true tenderness and care, the firelit, reflecting, feminine-held truth.

It was like those nights by the fire at the Sundance: I didn't want to go to sleep, didn't want it to end. But eventually it was time to call it, to let the fire burn out, and to crawl into our respective tents.

We were seated around the pit, the fire crackling and flickering. "Are you still going to walk and pray up in the buffalo pasture?" she asked, as I'd told her I did every time I was here in the land of my People, as I had the night before at the Sundance grounds. I was tired. I honestly wasn't going to. Our visit had been intense and full enough.

"I don't think so," I said. "I'm pretty beat. I'll have to give myself a raincheck on it."

"Really? I think you should."

"I don't know."

"You're here. You should."

I looked at her and felt the spirit of that old Sundancer get up. You do what you gotta do to see things through.

"All right, maybe I will."

We both got up. She went to her tent, and I stared back at the moonlit slope of the buffalo pasture. I was so proud of my People. I felt like we were so fucking awesome. We carried an inextinguishable cosmos inside of us and it didn't matter what anyone else said.

"Goodnight, Cliff," Chelsea said, her face in the half-zipped opening of her tent.

I smiled back at her.

"Goodnight, Chelsea. I'll see ya in the morning."

The wind blew over me and I started walking.

I walked through the line of unoccupied campsites over to the cattle-guard gate and climbed over it like I had dozens of times before. It was actually a little bright out with the moon and stars, so I didn't really need a flashlight to see. There was a vague road that ascended up the slope and my plan was to just walk up it, maybe to the pond or so, and then turn back. Walk, pray, listen, feel, and be grateful that I was still able to do these things as a Ponca on these lands. My spirituality didn't come from a book. It came from here, from my deep desire to know these generational realities of my People; and simple things like this, done often and regularly, were my practice. Here, there were spirits, and they were listening.

I walked up the road and felt so much invisible life interpenetrating the visible night; appreciatively, I walked as my stomach responded to what I was feeling, like a radar picking things up. I'd walked this road up to the sweat for years and years after our powwow ended on a Saturday night, seeing the big fire going, maybe one or two others standing around, getting things ready for everyone to go in about midnight (one time we opened the door between rounds and there was a buffalo just standing there behind the couple vehicles, looking directly at us). This was a road of memory. I loved it. I hoped I'd be walking it for decades and decades to come.

I continued walking up the slope, occasionally stepping around large, dried-out buffalo patties, praying and feeling, seeing as much as I could; like I was encountering a holy painting I knew I would never see again, so I'd better look at it as closely as I could while I could; this species of intensity always arose in me while I was up in my People's homelands. I walked and got about even with our small, compact sweat and, without going over to it, I checked it out, looking for signs of recent use, of which there were none. Then, like a doorway had opened in reply to my attention, I heard the spirits: *Come in here. We want to talk to you.* I stood looking at the covered-over sweat and could see that there were bodiless old people in there and they wanted me to literally crawl into that sweat with them then and there; to close the flap and bravely sit in the darkness with them so that they could talk to me some more. They said it again, like an invitation: *Come in here and sit with us. No*, I thought, *I'm not going in there.* I shuddered. I was spiritual and committed, but still young and apparently my fearlessness had its limits. I shook my head. Somehow, I was experienced enough with the spirits to know that it'd be okay if I declined. Not this time. Everything was wrapped in silence. I walked on and didn't look back at the sweat, the realness of what I'd heard trailing behind me. Whatever it was they had to show me, I guessed I wasn't ready for it yet.

I ascended the slope going toward the pond, eyeballing the ground, feeling the build-up of Spirit, praying aloud, doing my thing like the young person I was; making myself, making myself out of the experiences I wanted to be made of. And then I saw the buffalo: huge, semi-gathered on the back edge of the pond, awake and seemingly aware of me. I slowed and watched them, felt their immensity, their dangerousness, and imagined myself being the dumb Indian who pushed his luck and wound up trampled, dead on the hill. I stopped and watched them, didn't want to be that dumb Indian, talked to them some, their eyes looking in my direction, their forms shifting and turning, and then I turned around. That was as far as I was going to go tonight. I started heading back down, looking over my shoulder to make sure the herd wasn't following me, that I didn't need to hurry up and run. I walked and took in the expanse of Niobrara from that elevated vantage point, all of it a shimmering, unforgettable sight. My back prickled respectfully at our buffalo. I was one lucky Ponca.

I walked slowly down that vague road, feeling like I'd done my prayerful duty and my walk was coming to an end, looking at the black shadowy structure of the sweat and feeling okay with myself about not crawling in. And then, out of nowhere, I heard it begin to rain behind me. A light, soft rain up about where I'd turned around, pattering into the earth. I looked up but saw no clouds really, other than a few random ones; I couldn't even see the rain falling but could hear it clearly and so just kept on with my descent. I walked and prayed and heard the rain gaining on me, on course to swallow me up before I made it back to my tent, and I accepted it: some things there was just no outrunning. I didn't rush, could hear it percussively pelleting into the ground, and then when it was mere feet away, I just stopped to let it have me. I stood there, Sarah's SUV and our two tents not too far away now, the trees, the restrooms, earth lodge, and agency building all still and potent and dark, and then the rain spread beyond me, passing me, falling all around me, everywhere, but somehow, mysteriously, not actually on me at all. I stood there in that light, incessant rain, and was oddly, miraculously, dry as a bone.

It was the strangest, queerest thing. According to my ears, it was totally raining—I could hear it landing on the dry, grassy ground all around me—and yet, as I held my arms aloft and out, not a drop hit my skin, and actually, for the life of me, I couldn't see any rain at all. It was a peculiar, magical, sweet, powerful, unexplainable event created by the spirits to enfold me into some mysterious communication. I looked up and felt no rain on my face, smiled, felt a streak of happiness followed by streaks of something much deeper moving through me, like messengers arriving on the scene. I really couldn't believe it. I examined it, it didn't wane. I just stood in the middle of it and opened up like I knew how to, the pure-hearted beginner grateful to behold anything the Creator had to show him.

I began to pray and right away it was like a huge boundless mass of somethings began to assemble in the night air before me; a glimmering, a cosmic shape, a vision radiating into this world/my world in order to tell me something. What I saw visually is almost not as important as the degree to which my entire being was ecstatically engaged, and then the experiential comprehension I found myself traveling into. I saw all the infinite, distinct, unique essences of my Ponca tribe gathering and concentrating in the space in front of me, every iteration of our People's existence and every core essential spirit behind them, ornately convening and condensing into an overall communicative soul, allowing and giving me contact with my tribe's purest spirit and that purest spirit's every key, indispensable, precious manifestation. It was like all the stories that were uniquely Ponca in the cosmos, that comprised our Ponca cosmos, were unfolding and revealing themselves to me in that spirit-rain that was falling in our buffalo field. It goes without saying that there were more spirits and ancestors there in that nighttime field than anyone could've ever counted. The experience and my understanding of what was visiting me, kept growing and growing and I just surrendered to it, was struck open by the vision of this supernatural reality I'd never guessed I'd see in my lifetime: my Ponca People's All-Generating Divine Soul.

I watched it and felt it and prayed aloud to my ancestors, all the Elders and children and relatives inside of it, all the powerful caretakers and guardians and keepers present; that whole assembly/host who were there with me. I began to cry as I thanked them and reflected on the things I'd been given, the spirituality, healing, visions, medicine, friends, blessings, and closeness to the Creator that graced my life. I spumed with so many countless memories and just thanked them with my whole being for helping me to have such a good and beautiful life, even with all the wounds and suffering and loneliness and hardships that came with it. Overtaken by the peak-intensity of it all, I circled down into my core, where I was a writer and Sundancer living for the People, and spoke to them from there, my words alive and visibly moving into them, my prayers joining their transcendent multidimensional mosaic and form. I told them that I would do everything I could to take all that I'd been given by them and share it with our People so that everyone could have these blessings, the cultural and spiritual knowledge, the healing and enlightenment, the soulfulness and happiness, the health and well-being and wonder that was the birthright of all. I told them that this was my life's work as a writer and Sundancer and I promised the oceanic visionary composite presence before me that I would use my life to pass on all and everything that they had blessed my humble person with. I vowed to them that I would do this and just spiraled ever deeper into this truly ineffable sentient Ponca vista before me. I prayed and felt and vowed and the invisible rain continued to come down all around me.

Maybe about fifteen minutes passed and then I felt like I'd said all they needed me to say and they began to recede, winding back to wherever it was they actually resided; the night air thinning, layers lifting, things leaving. But that strange, light rain went on without ceasing. I stood there in the aftermath of that visitation and felt like I had a couple times before, like when I was driving to a motel in Yankton after coming down from the hill, or when I was back in Lincoln after Sundance. I felt the feelings of return, of coming back to the flow of your life after you'd gotten to see something about who you really were, why you were really here, after you'd been very, very close to the Sacred. And that rain wasn't going to stop. It was for me to leave it. I let myself have a few more long moments to really savor the dreamlike experience of it, the soul-marking gift of it, and then I let it conclude, saying my goodbyes, walking back down that road again. Soon, the rain was behind me; faint, not vanishing, but sure enough departing. I hopped that cattle-guard gate and went back to my tent, sleeping the sleep of a tired, happy man.

The next day we all three woke up and slowly got into the business of our morning, snacking on the fruit and granola and berries we had with us, wandering over one at a time to the restrooms to wash our faces and freshen up, and waving hello to the few Natives who were arriving for their work at the agency building, which housed our tribal museum and a couple other offices. I sat on the little worn bench and enjoyed the warmth of the sun on my body, loved getting to have another day with these unique and powerful ladies. I wondered what surprises would be in store for us today.

Eventually, we talked and planned and talked about coffee, and I volunteered to walk over to the agency building to see if I could round us up a few cups. I'd be lying if I said I didn't feel a little Indian pride, the usually unseen city Ponca now among his People and able to go and get some hot coffee from a cool tribal building all casually and just because. Sarah had already expressed to me that her little people helpers had told her that we were to be important friends and not romantic partners, and Chelsea had a fantastic, canoe-making boyfriend back in Washington, so I wasn't on a mission to impress that way but it still felt good for me to show them that I had a community to back up my character, that I really was essentially a good dude, and getting coffee for us all seemed like a good way to accomplish that. So, off I went.

I let myself in through the kitchen door and got to talking with a few folks in there, learning that they were preparing for a funeral (this was where we'd had our all-night wake for my grandpa Cliff Senior about seven years back and it was where many such family gatherings took place). I asked a big man with glasses who had passed, and he said, "It's a man they're bringing down from Wisconsin." My stomach tightened. I had a great uncle whom both my dad and I highly revered who lived in Wisconsin. "A man named Ronnie Picotte," he said. My heart dropped. That was him, that was my uncle. The night before when it was still all three of us by the fire and all the stories of being Ponca were spiriting out of me, I'd told them this story of my uncle Ronnie Picotte and this conversation we'd had just as I was leaving the powwow the year my dad had gone back to prison, getting ten years for dealing meth. It was an incredibly emotional conversation for me. He told me about the last time he'd talked with my dad at the casino, warning him, and he told me about the ceremony that had healed his cancer, about how I was supposed to live if I really was going to walk with a pipe. It was just him and me on a picnic table under the shelter on those very grounds, his two sons and my buddy Dan standing back and giving us space, me crying and listening, finally getting a chance to talk with some real family about my dad going away to prison. And now my uncle Ronnie was gone.

Indians feel so much because of all the spiritual sensitivity and connection we haven't lost, and it crushes us; it also maintains the generational lines and bridges that allow for our immortal ways to continue. We're good at living with this stuff, even when it kills us. I felt the unexpected event of my beloved uncle Ronnie's passing and carried on, hanging out with the workers in there for about half an hour, and then grabbing that coffee for my two guests and myself. I went back to our little campsite and told them what I'd learned, mentioning that he was the man from the story I'd told them the night before, without getting too deeply into the grief that was there, and they expressed their condolences. It was sad, rough, and we'd already cried so much; we drank our coffee and broke camp, resting in the energy of our endlessly beautiful Ponca homelands.

And there's really so much more to this whole story of the three of us, but I think I'll end it here. I was so in the habit of keeping my spiritual experiences to myself that it didn't even occur to me to try and take an hour to explain the transcendent visionary experience I'd had in the buffalo pasture to them; thirty-four years in conservative, rural Nebraska had not exactly groomed me into the kind of person/Indian who talked about their real spiritual life with all that much openness or ease. Such things swam down to the bottom of me where they could be safe, where their integrity could not be corrupted or fucked with; with many treasures coming from their safekeeping, such as this visit from Sarah and Chelsea and the spirits who were with them.

I had no idea, but in a handful of months my brother Clark would call me up, tell me that one of his roommates had abruptly moved out, and ask me if I'd be interested in moving to Seattle. Less than a month after that call, I'd liquidate everything, leaving that apartment I'd been in for fourteen years, my rad gas-station gig of ten years, selling my library of 1,500 books, leaving it all, and be on my way to Seattle. I feel like changes of such magnitude really only happen a couple times in a person's life; the change that has the power to rewrite everything. In Seattle, all my dreams were answered. In Seattle, I even found the one thing that had always eluded me, I even found love.

But all of that was still to come.

"I had a pipe once, but I couldn't carry it," my uncle Ronnie said, "so I gave it to this Medicine Man for him to have. If you're going to have a pipe, you're going to have to respect it, to really care for it. You've got to be true and know why you have it. Otherwise, it's not for you."

The powwow drum had everything rumbling and I wanted to hug him like a little boy, but instead I just listened like a young man.

I looked into his own teary eyes and then he continued on.

JACK BURTON AND THE MEDICINE MEN OF BEAR BUTTE

THE TWO OF THEM, my brother Denny's wife, Kelly, and her Ukrainian linguist friend, Vivi, had all their stuff laid out on the picnic table, semi-organized, to be taken in before it was all packed and crammed into their bikes somehow (or discarded and left behind). The three of us stood at our campsite there at Black Elk Peak, looking at it all after a long day of driving and picking things up, including their bikes, which they hadn't even ridden yet at all. We were in a bubble of firelight, surrounded by fresh, windy darkness.

"Wow. So, this is what it takes?" I asked, about five years older than the both of them, feeling a bit like a protective coach.

Kelly looked at me with a mixture of emotions on her face. "We hope so?"

The story so far: for the first time in ten years I'm jobless and enjoying more than just a single week off, in transit from Nebraska to Seattle, where I'm moving after thirty-five years of burrowing, digging, excavating, and living deeply in my home state. I spent four days staying with my poet-activist friend Amanda, went to our Sundance—my whole life shoved into my infamous Buick Roadmaster ("Now that's a rez car!")—then zipped off to the Badlands to meet Denny and his family at their Sundance, where we chilled and supported for three days, constantly in awe of the Martian landscape around us, and where I also learned that his wife had met this linguist at the Lakota Language Consortium about a month back and they both decided they were now best friends and, with no prior long-distance biking experience, were going to bike from Black

Elk Peak in South Dakota to LA together, setting off on what would've been the second day of the Sundance, for reasons of self-discovery, sisterhood, and joy. And they needed to borrow my car to run up to Rapid City to get their bikes and gather up all of their supplies. But the Sundance wound up being so affecting to them, especially to Vivi who had never been to one before, that they didn't wind up leaving until the last day and still weren't done going to all the places they needed to go to when we met up with them the day after that. So, I drove them all around Rapid in the Roadmaster, which had acquired a funky new sound under the hood after their using it for just that one day, and by the time we got to Black Elk Peak it was way too late for me to set off for Standing Rock, so it was decided that I'd stay with them in their tiny tent and see them off in the morning. My general read on their impulsive, epic bike trip was that they were super unprepared, ill-equipped, and inexperienced, and the more we drove around the more worried I became for them, but there was no turning back and so I didn't show it, instead I just focused on helping build up their mindsets and their confidence, adding what I could to the spirit of their launch. While we were shopping in Menards, a spirit told me to offer tobacco and pray for them every day of their journey until they reached LA. Internally, I nodded: message received.

It was crazy to me that they were going to ride these bikes that they hadn't even tested out yet all the way across half the country, and with about a hundred pounds of supplies strapped onto each of them. But what did I know? I was in the middle of what was maybe the biggest change I'd ever gone for in my life. What could I do but give them the encouragement I myself was hoping to receive from the people in my life.

"Tomorrow morning, we'll load up the bikes and whatever doesn't fit, you can take with you to Seattle," Kelly said, firm, fit, small, dark-haired; exactly the middle school reservation PE teacher that she was.

"Or maybe we can leave it here in a neat little pile on the picnic table for the next travelers to resupply with," I said, really in awe of the sheer heaping pile of it all.

"We could do that too," Vivi said, from over on the other side of the picnic table; slender, blonde, blue-eyed, and actually quite beautiful.

"Here, look at this," Kelly said, picking up and handing me a little beaded leather pouch. "My friend Josh who's staying with us made it for me to take on our trip."

I peered at the pouch in the dark, looking at the beaded picture on the front of it like a *Magic Eye* picture, like if I looked at it just right the whole thing might pop open for me.

"It has all the places of our upcoming journey on it," she said. "The Rocky Mountains, the desert, the ocean. Here, let's go over by the fire and you'll be able to see it better."

We went around the picnic table to the fire, and I held it up closer to my eyes, seeing now the zig-zag mountains and blue ocean that was singing in the beadwork; like a tiny Indian road map, hand-stitched and legitimately cool.

And then, as I was really looking at it, with Kelly quietly right beside me and Vivi across the fire from us, I was suddenly HIT/PELTED by some big softball-sized object right in my shoulder and hard as hell! Whatever had been hurled at me glanced off my shoulder and shot straight past Vivi, with all three of us seeing it clearly and entirely.

"What the fuck?" I reached for where I'd been hit—it was hard enough that I was totally going to have a bruise—and looked for where the object had landed, to see what it was.

"What was that!" Kelly asked.

"You saw it?"

"Yeah!"

"Did you see it, Vivi?"

Vivi was wide-eyed. "Yes."

The moment it hit me I knew it was a spirit that had thrown it, whatever it was. Our campsite was off on its own on the edge of things, with nothing behind us but raw forest for miles. We all looked back behind us and there was nothing but silence, darkness, trees, and night.

I held the pouch and asked Kelly, "What's in this pouch?"

"It's Josh's tribe's tobacco that he grew himself," she said. "He gave it to us for offerings."

"For offerings?"

She nodded.

"Hmm."

They were a little spooked and unsettled. I felt it too. There was more that I didn't understand than I did understand.

"That was a spirit that threw that," I told them.

"Like the little people?" Kelly asked.

"Naw, the little people might toss a pebble or a little stick at you to get your attention," I said, "but I've never had them blast me with anything like that."

"The spirits throw stuff like that?" she asked.

"I don't know. That was kind of crazy. Not usually. Do you see what it is that they threw?"

Vivi was looking down with the flashlight on her phone at where the object should've landed, but there didn't seem to be anything there, despite all three of us witnessing some actual physical thing ricocheting off my shoulder.

Vivi shrugged. "I don't see anything."

I held the pouch of tobacco: offerings for the spirits, blasted while I was holding it. There was so much to be afraid of in this world, but the spirits I walked with had taught me not to be afraid of anything, to be fearless like all good things were already a foregone conclusion and all things were ultimately all good things. My body was a little afraid, but I knew that I couldn't be. "I'm going to go pray," I told them, "and use some of this tobacco to make an offering."

Kelly seemed to be deferring to me in the same way that I was deferring to what I'd been taught. "Okay," she said.

I opened up the little pouch and took out a pinch of tobacco, holding it in my hand. I knew that I was supposed to go back to those woods behind us and pray, to where that projectile had come from. Walk up to them without any light and pray.

"All right," I said, looking at Kelly and Vivi, "I'll be back in a minute."

The next morning when I woke up, both Kelly and Vivi were gone. They'd told me that they planned to get up early so that they could go do a blessing ceremony of Kelly's tribe down at the water, as the last thing they really wanted to do before taking off. Sunshine filtered into the hot tent. When I'd gone up to the woods and prayed, I could feel that there were things listening to me; humility seemed my only recourse. Afterwards, talking a little more about it, I told them, "It just emphasizes how important it is to make your offerings and prayers along the way. You're going to be cared for and protected, but you've got to do your part." And then we kind of left it at that. It was pretty strange though, I'd never been blasted by a spirit like that before.

I sat in the tent, thought about reading one of the cool books Vivi had in there, but then I heard them coming back to the campsite area and got up and out, standing up into what was obviously going to be another sweltering day.

"Morning, Cliff!" Kelly said, wet and dripping, in her swimsuit with a towel around her waist.

"Morning. How was the water?"

Kelly was bright with life post-water ceremony. "Perfect. You should jump in quick if there's time."

"We'll see," I replied, thinking of the water and calculating my own travel plans. "Like you all, I've got quite a way to go and probably am better off getting on the road sooner rather than later."

Vivi ducked into the tent, Kelly dried her hair with the towel.

"We'll change, load up the bikes, and then get going," Kelly said, eyeing all the gear again.

I smoothed down my own wildman's mane and said, "Cool. Let me know what I can do to help."

We spent the next hour breaking camp and loading up the bikes; clipping the racks, saddlebags, and such on and then filling their every inch with all the food, bars, clothes, and living supplies they'd bought and brought. By the time both bikes were road-ready it was like they'd gone from the kind of bikes you'd ride across town on with your friends to some mega-badass machines you could take down to the tip of South America and back; they'd prepared and over-prepared and, supply-wise at least, weren't under-prepared. The first time Kelly hopped up onto her sleek two-wheeled ride, balancing on her tippy-toes and then clicking her special shoes into place on the pedals, she went forward just a few feet before wobbling and then totally falling over hard into the pock-marked pavement. It didn't look good; she couldn't even ride this bike a couple of feet and here she was planning on riding it all the way to LA. Again, I worried but didn't show it, as it was too late for that. I just tried to heart-emanate some pure encouragement her way. "You got this! You and your ride are one! LA is calling your name!"

We got them ready, tidied up our campsite, and then all three took off for the shop at the bottom of Black Elk Peak, hoping to get some coffee before we all got going our respective ways. They biked down, crashing a couple more times as they got the hang of it, and I drove, admiring the ancient beauty blanketing this sacred-place-turned-recreational-tourist spot. I took my time going down around the curves, looked at the other campers doing their morning things, the light coming down through the trees, the craggy rocks and boulders settled into their forever zones, the shimmering waters, and let myself get carried away some, feeling into what the Indians of the past must've felt when they entered into this mountain's presence. It was a gift to even try to catch a taste of the things the Old Ones knew. I cruised with the windows down, smiling and wondering when I'd ever get to come back here again.

Down at the shop we chatted with the clerk, poked around the souvenirs (I saw the exact carved wooden buffalo that Clark, my soon-to-be roommate in Seattle, had sent me a few years earlier, saying he'd found it at a thrift store and thought of me; that was kind of a cool moment), and got our scalding hot and delicious coffee. We went outside and sipped our soul-fuel, lazing and lingering in the space of our inevitable goodbye: from the grand sacred ceremony of the Sundance, to our comically running around Rapid, to our night together at Black Elk Peak with the supernatural happening, and then to this shared departure point on our pair of epic journeys to the West Coast. Time can carry so much; twenty-four hours can feel like an entire novel. We enjoyed our coffee, rocked back and forth on our heels in the parking lot.

"Let me know when you make it," I said, feeling a sort of fullness as I looked at these two committed young women. "I myself should be in a whole different life by the time you do."

"We'll take pictures," Vivi said, "and send them to you. Anything cool we come across you'll be seeing on that cool little flip phone of yours."

We all kind of laughed.

"Thanks for saying my flip phone is cool, Vivi. It really means a lot."

We all finally hugged and really said our goodbyes and then I watched them bike off, shrinking away, not falling, secure with each other and empowered by their fiery, new, transformational friendship; a pair of women on a trip together that they'd both surely remember for the rest of their lives.

And then I got into my Roadmaster—packed with all my earthly belongings—and set off for Standing Rock, eager to meet up with Denny and the kids, chock-full of goodness, poetry, and jazzy coffee.

"Standing Rock is only five hours away," I thought, kind of gunning it. "I should get there with time to spare."

I sat in the roadside diner's parking lot, shaking off some of the sideways looks I'd gotten inside, slurping my soda and poring over the large analog map spread across my passenger seat. I really did just have a flip phone and had never used Google Maps in my life. Charting my path, I saw how close I was going to be passing by Bear Butte; I'd practically graze its outer edge. I was tired and didn't know when I'd ever be in the area again, and I'd always told myself that I'd visit that holy mountain again someday. I unwrapped my cheeseburger and looked down at the lines and colors of the map. "Bear Butte?" I asked, taking a bite. "Do I really have the time?"

I'd first visited Bear Butte when I was about twenty-five, finding myself with an extra day before I had to go back to work after coming down from the hill and deciding to seize my chance to visit that sacred place, as like a part of my ravenous drive to continue growing my personal knowledge of the larger cosmic framework my People were situated in (also, I'd never seen the Black Hills and thought I could drive through them too). It turned out to be a long round-trip I did not regret. I drove across the center-line of South Dakota, almost ran out of gas in the Badlands, was puzzled by and then began to laughingly appreciate the infinite WALL DRUG signs, made it to Sturgis and got myself a cheap motel room, where I processed and recovered from my fast while pondering what Bear Butte was going to be like the next day. I fell asleep remembering things I'd heard: Fools Crow literally walking into the side of the butte, emerging with stones embedded beneath his skin that moved around and were alive; Joe Bad teasing an old drinking buddy of his who'd become a Medicine Man and was putting some people up to fast, who got irked when Joe called him by an old nickname in front of his supporters; Ken Bordeaux putting out hard candies on the fenceposts there and then watching the little people come down to retrieve them in the early hours of the morning.

The next day when I went there, I wound up having an experience myself while sitting on the little platform at the top, prayer ties speckling the scrappy trees around me. I was alone and singing a song when I heard the spirits tell me to leave the necklace I was wearing behind as an offering. It was a special necklace for protection that I'd been given by an older friend of mine who'd imbued it with his own gift, a gift that I had much respect for. It was a hard thing to part with, but the spirits' instructions were clear and I trusted them. Such things were irreplaceable, but they also all had their role to play in the overall scheme of one's life-ceremony. When I was done singing, I scrambled down into the trees and tightly tied the black and white necklace to the branch of what seemed like a very sturdy, out-of-the-way tree; and then I told myself that if it was still there whenever I came back someday that I'd untie it and take it back, kind of like what the hell, if you know what I mean. Later, Denny would tell me, "They say that when you go to Bear Butte you're supposed to bring offerings, but not just normal stuff; you're supposed to bring something that's really important and meaningful to you and offer that. That's why the spirits had you leave that necklace. The protocol was fulfilled even if no one ever told you about it."

(I think that maybe when you do that, follow that particular protocol, you sort of leave a small piece of yourself there and remain forever heart-connected to that holy, innermost center of our People's land and cosmos; your prayer tie looped into the ever-growing bundle that's been there since the beginning. And you FEEL this. That butte and whatever it houses becomes permanently alive in you. Maybe, probably, it's something like that.)

So, ten years later and with my route taking me right past it, I had to make a detour and stop there. *Maybe I can get my necklace back*, I chuckled and thought to myself, throwing a ketchupped fry down the hatch. *Maybe it's survived four-thousand-some days of weather and it's still there waiting for me.*

I powered up the Roadmaster, wheeled back onto the highway, and got going. I was ready to sleep in a real bed for the first time in days, but all in due time. I was like an Indian Jack Burton from *Big Trouble in Little Nebraska*: my rig and I had some serious business to attend to.

I scarfed down my lunch and drove toward the vast presence that was Bear Butte.

The Roadmaster bucked and roared and skipped. It was a hundred degrees out, and I drove with the windows down; we never used the air conditioning in our car when I was a kid and as an adult I continued this tradition. Hot as hell, I flew down the road.

I passed through Sturgis, site of America's largest motorcycle rally every year, and remembered all the bikers I'd seen everywhere the last time I went to Bear Butte, remembered the raunchy camcorder footage my horror filmmaker buddy's biker dad had shown us in high school when he'd returned from the rally. Recently, I'd been following articles in the newspaper about the huge road-house concert venues they wanted to build at the base of the butte to make their millions; all the Indians doing their ceremonies and making their pilgrimages be damned. Commerce and Capitalism raged to consume everything, with anything that was sacred to us Indians fully designated as prime targets. Christ tapping away on his iPhone at the Sundance, you know?

I left Sturgis behind, following my passenger seat's map, and aimed for the mountain, appreciating the colors and character of the terrain, feeling the dual flow of twenty-first century civilization and the older, living conversations comprising all the layers of Indian Country; like ancient redwoods submerged in some strange CGI static. I rattled along, drove safely, didn't pass anybody, sensed all the spirits who were tending to all the things people were coming from near and far to connect with. To my left, the butte cropped up in my vision. I made my turn, felt the telling quiet. I wasn't exactly anybody special, but looking at the butte I could see how the whole story of our species was all about our relationship to the Sacred, with a huge part of that written and embodied by our Mother Earth Herself. Every story was really the story of that relationship and its infinite variations, and how off-course things went when we forgot the centrality of that relationship. Our Indian culture was saturated with this relationship and that was why we'd always have our Black Elks and Fools Crows; that was why the crystal compass in our souls would always bring us back to Bear Butte.

I drove up the smooth road to the parking lot and tourist shop at the base of the butte, sweaty and tired and robed in an energy of homecoming. I always felt like other Natives were always showing up to things with other Natives, but I was always rolling up alone; I wanted it to be different, but this kept being my way. There was no one waiting for me there with a cold Pepsi and a good laugh, just other folks looking over my pony-tailed self, trying to read my motivations and how on-the-level I was. I parked, rolled up my windows, sucked down the dregs of my fountain pop till it wheezed, and then got out and locked things up. Should I look directly or not? I turned toward the mountain and looked.

Bear Butte wasn't chiseled with a classic peak but rather was scrubby, old, full of breadth, covered with small trees, colored like the rest of the spartan, former sea-bottom land of South Dakota. In my humble imagination I saw it as an ancient entity before entities had faces, when their overall forms served that expression function in a somehow far more sophisticated manner; I saw an old grandma who was cooking medicine soup for all and everyone who needed an old Indian grandma of the North American variety; I saw a misty Miyazaki fantasy realm swirling with softness and light, hardness and endurance, all geared toward ceremonies and doings that both predated and post-dated this current so-called America; I saw something immovable, perpetually expressing the reality of communion, and slightly irritated. A single delineated trail cut up to its top from the end of the parking lot, which was about a two hour-plus round-trip hike. The last time I'd climbed to the top I'd felt like I was perched inside some dreamworld lens, being spiritually rewoven as I contemplated the 360-degree view of the surrounding land. The smoke of me blending with the smoke of thousands of generations of relatives who'd reverently viewed the earth-body of our Mother from that same, hallowed spot. It was a blessing. All that and then more, times a million, wrapped in the rock of that sacred mountain.

I walked up to the trailhead and, practically speaking, didn't really feel like I had the time for a couple-hour hike to the top and back this trip. I looked at all the colorful prayer ties that were tied up everywhere and decided I'd maybe go and check out the area that was non-public and reserved for ceremonial purposes, the area I'd just briefly walked around some that last time. But first I knew that I'd better go pay my respects to Fools Crow and offer him some tobacco, so I moseyed over to the tourist building where his stately, lifelike bronze bust was, all wrinkled and alive like he was really looking at you, and put down a pinch of Bugler tobacco on the podium rim where everyone else had left their cigarettes, ties, and offerings. I'd dreamed of that old holy man when I was younger. All the leaders of my dance (three brothers, all a year apart) had started out dancing with him when they were just boys. I prayed and talked to him as a few people walked past me into the building, feeling less self-conscious than the last time when I'd done the same thing. He was of another era, but also still very much here. I looked into his face. "You came back," I imagined him saying. "Good job, Grandson. Good job."

I walked the more private path kind of down and around the side of the butte, alone and seeing no one, crossing a wooden footbridge and then emerging into a space where I could sense a different character of activity present. I had no expectations, really just to pray some, remember, and visit wherever my feet took me, kind of like almost ceremonially bathing myself in Bear Butte's energy just like Kelly and Vivi had done in that lake back at Black Elk Peak. The time to see if my necklace had managed to hang on for me at the top would have to wait. I felt like I had an hour max and that was about it.

The path began to open up some, and I could hear that there were other people over here on this side, actually quite a number of them. I slowed down, kept walking and looking around, and then, tucked back amidst a warped gray wall of gnarled trees, I saw a pair of guys sitting beside a dead campfire on some nylon chairs, their small tents behind them. I paused and turned toward the louder collection of voices quite a way farther up and saw what looked like a post-ceremony celebratory feast with all sorts of reservation Natives laughing and teasing and sort of just blissfully being together. I recognized both parties, the group and the pair: the group was that Sundance family, that tiyospaye, and the pair was like me, a couple of lone wolves on a mission. I didn't have the zest or the courage to just walk up to the wild howling cake-eating family with their awnings and tables and flowing love, but I was experienced enough in the lone-wolf ways to go and talk to the two quiet guys. I was fluent with them, while still working on my fluency with the others.

I walked up to the pair of dudes and introduced myself, instantly catching a few things: they both looked white but probably weren't; there was about a ten-year age difference between them and a teacher-student dynamic vaguely present; and they reminded me of the older, roughed-up-by-life neighborhood customers from my gas station who were always mostly friendly beneath their toughened exteriors. Nervous as I was, I knew we'd get along just fine.

"My name's Cliff. I'm Ponca from Nebraska," I told them. "I'm on a road-trip to Seattle, where I'm moving. I'm heading to Standing Rock to visit my brother for a week, but thought I'd stop by here first since it was on the way. This is only the second time I've ever been here."

The older guy looked exactly like some perfectly cast hippie Native from a '70s movie, like a cross between Billy Jack and a jean-jacketed guy on his way to Crow Dog's Sundance, if they'd ever made a movie about that. He was shaggy, strong looking, had a thick face, and eyes that had earned their squint and their light. He pointed to a cooler. "Have a seat if you'd like."

I semi-cooly, semi-awkwardly entered their cluttered little campsite and sat down on the closed cooler, just like I'd done with my dad when I was kid and we went fishing. The other guy, slower to speak, maybe in his late forties to the older one's late fifties, light-skinned, short, night-black hair, a touch sad, his life never going as planned but now kind of used to it, pulled out some tobacco from his chair's pocket and held it up. "Wanna smoke?"

I'd been trying to quit for years but it worked so well at speeding-up the friend-making process between strangers that I nodded and said sure. He tossed me the tobacco and I caught it, got to rolling myself a cigarette.

We all started talking, the older guy telling me his tribe, which didn't ring a bell; the younger guy saying he was Ojibwe, which felt right; how they were on a long summer trip visiting friends and sacred sites; how that other group was wrapping things up after two young men had completed their fasts; and I kind of fumbled and fucked-up and made a horror show of my cigarette, spilling my tobacco all over like I was drunk or blind or both. It was kind of good and funny. "You need some help with that?" the younger guy asked sincerely and respectfully. No magical cigarette rolling powers did I have; my youth fully betraying itself, I again said sure.

The younger guy rolled me a smoke, handed it to me, and then I lit it up, crumbling into goodness and that subtle, crackling edge that indicated the spirits. We ended up talking for about forty-five minutes, speaking of the little people, things the older teacher-ish guy was taught by his teachers, laughing quite a bit, and then even gracefully pausing our conversation when the Medicine Man of that big group came down, shook our hands (I'd actually heard about him for years but had never met him; he didn't look like I'd imagined at all, didn't have the bearing I was used to or expected either), gifted the older guy with a yuwipi rattle from their weekend's proceedings, explaining what was inside of it and how he could use/care for it, and then busted everything wide open by telling us this utterly nuts real-life story about the night before when his helper accidentally POOPED HIS PANTS while going to check on the two guys fasting, and how their whole camp practically detonated and CRAPPED THEIR PANTS when that helper very shamelessly came literally crawling back down without having finished his task and told them all why. It wasn't the kind of conversation any non-Indian would probably imagine a circle of four sweaty Indians having on the side of a sacred mountain right after an object of true spiritual power had been gifted, but it was also exactly the kind of humor and wild-ass talk us Indians were always having after ceremony and otherwise. My water bottle ranneth over. The Medicine Man returned to his family, everyone breaking everything down, and then they all left, leaving just the three of us and our cigarettes.

Then something very crazy and cinematic happened.

While all three of us were swimming in all the stories we were telling, this absolutely deafening wind shot down from the butte and drowned out our every word for a few very long seconds. It was like a different signal canceling out our tiny human voices, filling our world with a distinctive, attention-grabbing, powerful ROAR, and we all stopped talking until it passed. When it was done, we all just looked at each other, the expressions on our faces that of three Natives who had all really witnessed something incontestably supernatural flashing through our midst.

The older guy, tanned, unshaven, wearing his headband, and with much seriousness to him, looked off into the direction of where that wind had come from, like some deep perception or reasoning was turning in him, and then he said, "I gotta go."

Neither the younger guy nor I said anything. The older guy got up, ducked into his tent, got his pipe bag, and then, without saying anything more, stalked off up the butte, very quickly disappearing from our view.

"That wind was probably a sign, huh?" I asked the younger guy.

He looked like the kid who shadowed the slightly-off but heroic guy he always wanted to be like; the one that would let him shadow him anyway.

"Definitely," he said, reaching for a pack of smokes from a bag by his feet.

"You ever seen him do that before?"

"No. But he's told me stories."

I looked at his cigarette.

"Could I have one?"

The air was still and hot.

I lit my cigarette.

And then there were two.

The Ojibwe guy and I smoked and talked, everyone else gone, Bear Butte all leather and rock and grass with pieces of an ancient heaven hidden and humming within. I still had a couple hours of driving ahead of me, but there was no need to leave until it felt natural to do so. Plus, I truly enjoyed the cigarettes and this slice of real and potent Indian life I'd bumped into.

I told him some more about my life, a sketch of what was going on in my head as I transplanted myself to Seattle, how tough it was to leave everyone back home, my gas station poet's life, and he told me about his kids, mistakes he'd made over and over again, his drinking and partying days, the sort of Native life story stuff I'd not only heard and been around my whole life but was actually the child of, which touched me because of just how much personal and collective history is packed and writhing inside our stereotypical Native pains and problems; because of the unutterable ocean of grief that is the actual source of all our bad choices and decisions. But then we got to talking about the present-day, the things that made us into the kinds of Natives who found themselves at Bear Butte. I told him about my being a Sundancer, how committed I was to the Red Road, and then, sinking back into his biography, he came out with his own story of the Sundance. I smoked my cigarette and listened. Whenever someone in the wild, or the mainstream civilian world, started talking to me about their experience with the Sundance, I always tried real hard to catch their every word because it was like that grand ceremony itself that was hugging and carrying us all was speaking directly to me, telling me one more thing that it wanted to have permanently and blessedly lodged in my soul's memory. Time and conversation became palpably charged. It was like that children's book, but much more high-stakes and crucially real: *All I Really Need to Know I Learned from the Sundance.*

"When I finally quit drinking my kids were already out of my life," he said, smoking, looking down, looking at me. "I got a job at the casino and that was pretty good. I liked the people there. But I started thinking about the Sundance. I had some Lakota friends who were Sundancers, but I'd never been to a dance myself. I kind of wondered if we Ojibwe had ever had a Sundance, and eventually I went and talked to my grandpa and he said that the Sundance was a part of our history, that we used to have them too. Then one day, my boss, Janice Bad Moccasin—"

When he said Janice Bad Moccasin something in my chest slid open: Janice was Joe Bad Moccasin's cousin, and Joe was the Medicine Man I danced my first two years with when I was twenty-two. My first year with Joe in Crow Creek, Janice actually had her own dance on the same property that had splintered off from Joe's, and that dance was finishing up its last day during our first day of purification. No words passed through my mind or left my mouth. I just kept listening.

"—started talking to me about the upcoming summer and my plans and then her plans, and then she told me that she was going to her cousin's Sundance and had to get things ready for that. I really perked up then and told her that I'd been curious about the Sundance, about how I talked with my grandpa about it. Next thing you know, she asked me if I wanted to come. I was all about it. Here I was interested and then suddenly I'm getting invited to one. We had a lot of sweats and pretty soon instead of just going, I was planning on dancing. The months flew by. Then it was summertime and we all went to Cousin Joe Bad Moccasin's Sundance."

I heard Joe's name in that blazing sun on Bear Butte and felt ol' Grandpa Joe at the campsite with us; these Medicine Men and Elders help us and then remain unforgettably with us, more valuable than any of the stuff that people are compromising themselves for every day. The culture and medicine streamed through Joe; those same forces that originally birthed and built our Native cultures, that protected our sacred mountains, MOVED through him. With Joe gone several years now, I listened. Hearing about him from a stranger on Bear Butte, so far away from the home I was leaving and the one I was heading to too.

"The Sundance, well, you know, was tougher than I'd imagined. I met a lot of good people there. There was a lot of spirituality there. It was inspiring. It was scary. Joe was a good man, kind, really nice to me even though he didn't know me."

He changed, remembering something. He seemed to slump down just the tiniest little bit. I wanted to tell him that I knew Joe, that the very Sundance he was talking about was where I first danced, but I also wanted to let him continue talking, to get out the full story of what he was sharing. This was a medicine synchronicity orchestrated by the spirits to give me a much-needed sign about my faith and what was guiding/bringing me to Seattle, but I didn't need to interrupt him and tell him that; I just needed to say, "I know what you're talking about. I've been there too," but in a minute, in a minute.

He continued on.

"I can't remember which but on the second or third day, Joe came over to me and said he had a request. He told me that he'd had a couple heart attacks and couldn't pierce anymore and then he asked me if I would pierce for him that year. I actually wasn't planning on piercing. They told me I could just pierce on one side if I wanted to or not at all. I don't think I was ready. It was hard to be there with Joe in that moment. I could see how much he wanted to, he just didn't have the health for it anymore; it was too dangerous for him. I told Joe, 'I'm going to have to decline. I'm sorry.'"

A wisp of dusty sadness whirled through him. I was a bit surprised that he didn't step up, but also didn't blame him; each of us is on our own journey and you have to respect that.

"I only danced that one year. Kind of got back into drinking for a couple years after that. I'd love to go back someday. Still have three years left of my commitment. But I like how things are going now. I like helping my friend, learning from him. I'm doing a lot of stuff on the reservation for our youth now. It's more fulfilling than any night of drinking ever was. It's good work. To help our youth have a different life than we did."

I looked at the dead campfire and drew on my cigarette, felt many scenes and times nesting into this conversation, this man's recollection of the one and only Sundance he'd ever been to, of Joe Bad and his piercing request. This was like getting blasted by the spirits too, but in an eternity-spun, heartening way. I often felt like I was an employee of the ancestors, one of their agents in the field; and here they were showing me again that whatever message they had to get to me they'd get to me, period. My heart, carved of the world in which they lived, would always hear them. You could see that he felt good sharing his story of the Sundance, that it had centered him in his soul; I kind of smiled at him and told him my part.

"You know where I danced my first two years at?"

He looked at me, waiting.

"At the same place. The Hunkpati Oyate Wiwang Wacipi. At Joe Bad Moccasin's Sundance. It must've been just a couple of years after you were there. Crazy, huh?"

"Really?" he asked, the whole thing slowly dawning on him.

"Yup. What are the odds? I never would've guessed in a million years that during my short stop at Bear Butte I'd end up having a conversation with someone else who'd Sundanced with ol' Joe Bad back in the day, with that Medicine Man who forever changed my life. I'm really glad I came here today."

He looked at me like he was filling up with some of that light that was permeating the mountain.

"So am I," he said. "I'm glad that we've met too."

I pulled out of the Bear Butte parking lot and got the Roadmaster back on the road, hitting seventy and rocketing along in no time. That older guy was still gone when I finally took off, doing whatever prayerful, '70s-hippie-film Native thing that big wind had compelled him to do; chances were, I'd probably never see him again but who knew. I'd gotten the other guy's mailing address and told him I'd send a copy of my little people book, and I really wanted to: I wanted to communicate to him the largeness of that Joe Bad Synchronicity and I thought that my book, which was dedicated to Joe, could really stamp it with some power like that. I looked at the road signs and felt the deathly summer heat blowing over me through the open windows, drove with one hand and let the other grab at and shake in the wind. Seattle was still a long way away.

It was hard to believe that it hadn't even been twenty-four hours since Kelly and Vivi and I were all looking at the hundreds of items spread across the picnic table that they were intending to bundle onto their brand-new bikes. By now they were at least fifteen or twenty miles closer to California, probably pretty tired, sunburned, swarming with thoughts of how they were going to make it, how they were going to glide into the welcoming arms of their sweet, final destination. I reminded myself to stop off and pray and offer some tobacco for them somewhere before I pulled into Denny's for the night, to do my part as I said I would and make my contribution. When I got to Denny's I'd probably also get my first update, hear how their day went and what field or motel they were sleeping in that night. Their epic journey running concurrent with mine was almost a little comforting; because we were both doing it, it seemed that much more real that it could be done. I could work with that. Heck, now that I thought about it, maybe they were even praying for me.

I sped along and thought about Joe, the years of ceremony, friendship, and Sundancing with him, the moments and conversations, palling around with his family, watching him get sicker, his laughter and personality persisting in a sort of trademark manner even as his body failed him more and more; how he rubbed his hands together like a hungry villain and said, "This is going to be a good one," and then everyone would laugh because we all knew that it was. How proud he was of me, how kind; the twenty-one-year-old shy, skinny Ponca quietly bursting with passion and tears over the continent of sacred ancestral culture that he was waving me over and guiding me into. I knew a Medicine Man when I was young and he helped me find my moccasins, haha. Really though. His name was Joe Bad Moccasin, and he helped me find my moccasins.

I roared forward in my dad's old drug-dealer car and the road really did look like a thing designed to take me to where the spirits wanted me to go; bombed-out, heat-miraged, echoing with the travels of all those who came before me. I'd done a lot to get to the skin I was in now, to get to this shining point. I couldn't imagine what was next and somehow everything about that felt just perfect.

I howled down the road and embraced it.

GRANDPA SAMMY IN NEW ORLEANS

I WAKE UP ON OUR couch, sweaty and semi-rested, see that it's almost six o'clock, and go about my reasoning. Aislinn is down in the French Quarter and by seven-thirty she should know if she's getting a tour—she's a ghost tour guide for the hordes of tourists—or not; if not, she'll be free and ready to meet up and catch some dinner or whatever. If I go to Café Envie now, I'll have about half an hour to read and get some coffee-shop time in. If she gets a tour, then I'll just have more time. I sit up and look at our messy, cluttered living room, high-five all the spirits that must be there, pull my shoes on, grab my stuff, and get the hell out the door.

I step outside and some New Orleans atomic sunshine tries to melt my face off, making my knees wobble a bit. I unlock my bike from our railing and carry it down the stairs, smiling at the two kids who're playing next door, and then send a head nod over to their drunk, glassy-eyed dad on the porch. "You going to meet your lady?" he lobs down, his words like some sticky stuff that loses all its shape mid-air.

"Yup," I answer. "Time to take the horse down to the Quarter and meet up with her."

"All right," he says, dropping his neck like someone just pulled his power cord from the socket for a second and then plugged him back in. I throw my shoulder bag on and get biking over the cracked sidewalk and into the cratered street. My horse flies. Time to get!

Aislinn always takes the safer route of the neutral ground that adds about five extra minutes to the trip, but I just cut straight through the belly of our neighborhood, St. Roch, fearless for all sorts of reasons that can be very eloquently summed up as JUST BECAUSE. I often see a woman named Turvy biking around who was attacked while on her bike and beaten to the point of brain damage. The week before I moved down here, Aislinn was robbed by a bunch of kids while on her bike and I was in Seattle on the other end of phone, utterly in love, like, *What neighborhood am I moving into? Is it even safe?* My coworker at the African restaurant in the Quarter, D, an ex-con who'll later overdose while on the clock (I'll have to convince my boss to call 911; it's crazy), upon hearing where we lived, said, "St. Roch? I'd never live there. I was born and raised here and that's the most dangerous neighborhood in New Orleans." I bike past all the overgrown lots, other shotgun apartments, candy-colored houses, ruined fortresses, and just emanate my field of peace, wave at some old dudes I see all the time, wonder at some of the more hermetically sealed homes, taking the center of the street, swerving, and trying not to get hit when a car comes. I was looking for love my whole life and then I finally found it and it brought me to New Orleans. Moral: you never know where the hell love's going to take you. Never.

I stop for traffic at St. Claude, our nearest main street, breathe for a second, spot a heavily tattooed goth queen in a cape and appreciate her liberated magic, and then I zip across into the Marigny. It's a total vibe-shift. Things are nicer, softer, safer. I coast over spray painted Katrina-era symbols that're like dark memories and worms of emergency frozen into the asphalt. When I first moved here, we watched a documentary about Katrina and it showed the street we lived on in St. Roch flooded up to the tops of the street signs; ten years later, the trauma is still fresh and the city is far from rebuilt. I pass Who Dat Coffee and then curve around the Orange Couch, a coffee shop I love that has an actual orange couch, both places we visited when Aislinn first took me around. I check out the mixture of hipsters and gutter-punks out front, nod to a few of them, feel the love that sometimes flashes between strangers here, that NOLA electricity howling like a hundred thousand warrior celebrators defending the city shores against every colonizing force that would eventually take over. Cotton candy bubbles of nourishing light issue in response from the Orange Couch and break against me, cooling and encouraging me. I peddle through this ornate puzzle box zone of history and loved-life on the edge of the (in)famous French Quarter and feel bothered, blistered, tired, elated, powered-up, powerfully Ponca, and unique. The draw of the city is instantly understandable to anyone with the right soul make-up and to most without it. Chin-up megaton artistic expression in the smoking wreckage of cannibalistic American progress is the name of the game around here. Magic, music, plants, dance, ceremony, madness, resilience, struggle, Mardi Gras. I bullet into the Quarter and see a gathering of homeless people in the park, a sparkling pink mime surrounded by onlookers, a boy sleeping peacefully on the sidewalk with his big wolf-dog.

The energy of the Quarter is unmistakable, flaming over me, flooding into my system. Romance, grit, dreams, dancing in the night with new friends you'll never forget. TOURISTS: coming for the experience, the escape, some good-natured, some grinding their teeth for release and sin. I feel all my friends here: the baristas, the guitar-playing Native intellectual (Atakapa-Ishak Nation), the blue-haired poets, fierce waitresses who talk to me about their plants, Aislinn's and my spirit-family, who've engulfed us with love from the start. People I canoe with, watch heart-rending Native documentaries with, sweat with, talk dreams with, saw at Standing Rock when the shit was going down, attended tapings of *The Moth* podcast with, performed at a fundraiser for L'eau Est Le Vie with, where the battle against the Black Snake continues. An unkillable love is at the geometric center of this city and all these folks have clipped themselves into it, sourcing their very human lives from it. I crack open with joy and share it with the bustle and pedestrians and hungry droves and cars surrounding me. Wild that a kid from Nebraska wound up living in such an epic, storied city; I'm like a thirty-something writer in love straight out of the movies. I weave around everyone and slow at the corner in front of

Cafe Envie, take in the chess players and other characters outside, lock my bike up to one of the chipped black columns. I say hey to a husky brother I know who's both a Trekkie and a carpenter, and then head on in.

I get a cup of coffee and post up at a table along the wall, allow myself to plant down, to pull back into my own world some. I get out my notebook and the fat Jodorowsky graphic novel I'm reading, set my things up, relax into this writing/reading/dreaming routine that I've been running for twenty years, preparing to float off and spend some quality time on this other planet of pure inspiration and soul. With my coffee and the tools of my trade, there are an infinite number of utterly beautiful places I can go. I can visit the spirits, the past, healing realms, the poetry ocean, the dreamworld. I sip my coffee and space off. Minutes slip by people-watching and a small stone of gratitude travels the maze of me right into my core. I look at my phone and see that it's about six-thirty; no texts or updates from Aislinn. My mind becomes silent, and I sink happily into the watching, experiencing the carnival, feeling exactly where I'm at in the story of my life. Then, unbidden, I begin to think about Grandpa Sammy.

Grandpa Sammy Little Owl: hitchhiking with his nephew Tim in the early '80s, crisscrossing the Dakotas doing family medicine work, backpacks, cigarettes, offerings, pipes, locating and visiting and fasting at a buried network of half-destroyed sites numbering in the high thousands, conversing with ancestors who literally lived in the unassuming sites like immortal Indians of old living in ageless tipis. A tiny snapshot of my brother Denny's deceased grandpa who we always jokingly/not jokingly say is like our Yoda. I feel him and drink my coffee; it's like these thoughts of Sammy are playing a very specific song on the instrument of my heart, calling up memories of those forces that eternally maintain themselves as the shapers of life, of people's lives, a river's life, a mountain's life, a civilization's life. I feel the interior nature of those forces and wonder at a human's capacity to do so. Grandpa Sammy left the earth about fifteen years ago, was a schoolteacher, a Medicine Man, a song-keeper, and many more things, and is alive to this day in ways we're all still finding the words for. On an average day, he was visited by ghosts, grandmas, rock stars, and bright-eyed kids alike. He's a legend. I feel the luck of having him in my life, in my dreams, by my side, and then I find myself spinning my phone in a kind of circle with my finger, looking at its blank screen. And then it hits me: I should Google Grandpa Sammy! He's been a part of my life for going on eleven years and everything I know about him comes from the stories Denny's told me and experiences I've had with him, and never once has it occurred to me to look him up on the internet to see if there's anything about him in such a common, mundane place. Who knows why I never thought to search for him online before. He was a real, regular person after all. I pick up my phone and type his name into the search bar, press ENTER, and wait a second to see what happens.

Nothing comes up. Practically nothing. It's both a relief and the tiniest fanboy disappointment (make no mistake, among other things, I am a fucking fan of Sammy!). A lean obituary. An unrelated children's book. And then . . . wait . . . a Google Books result! I click on the link and begin to read: "at the University of Nebraska, there were eight hundred or so human remains classified as culturally unidentifiable, and the agreement provided that the university would recognize a shared group relationship between those human remains and the signatory Indian nations. Repatriation is also a sovereignty issue, and that fact gives Indian nations a say in the disposition of human remains.

"After that agreement was reached, a working group of tribal representatives began a long process over several meetings to determine what we would do with those remains. What tribal group or groups would rebury them? Where would we put them back into Mother Earth? At one point, we sought spiritual guidance. Sammy Little Owl, a Mandan, Hidatsa, and Arikara from North Dakota, agreed to conduct a ceremony. He has an ability to communicate with our ancestors. Following the ceremony, Sammy said that a number of excited children had run up to him, followed by a leader who said they had lived on a high bluff overlooking the Missouri River and that was where they wanted to be reburied.

"Thankfully, the Northern Poncas agreed to share their land for the reburial. Near Niobrara, Nebraska, in 2002, we returned our ancestors to Mother Earth in a site very similar to the one Sammy had described to us. The cemetery sat on a bluff overlooking the Missouri and Niobrara Rivers.

"A reburial is a spiritual undertaking. It is done with the greatest reverence, and it brings joy to us because we know that we have removed the spirits of our ancestors from those places where they've been incarcerated, and that we are putting them back into the womb of Mother Earth where they belong. While filling the grave with earth near Niobrara that day, we looked up and saw an eagle flying in circles, going up and up and up until it disappeared."[2]

WHAT THE FUCK? I look around for a witness, see a painted man in a blue suit staggering along, a neon-green-haired girl doing yoga on the sidewalk; not a witness in sight. My heart beats fast and I drink some more coffee. Again, HOLY SHIT! For over a decade I lived just a couple blocks away from UNL and my buddy Rick, the son of Ken Bordeaux, had several times told me all about the shameful, ignominious things the anthropology department there had been up to with our People's bones and remains. And for that same decade plus, every time I would go to visit the Ponca cemetery that was referenced, I would walk around praying and putting tobacco on different graves, including this monument marking where all of these relatives were ultimately repatriated and reburied. Grandpa Sammy was who they called in to talk to the ones bound to those bones at UNL, and the leader who came and told him where to bury them was an Old Ponca! New Orleans shudders in all her screaming historic glory and I marvel at this way that Sammy was intersecting with all of these soul-lines of my own life way before I ever learned of him,

[2] See James Riding In's essay, "Protecting Native American Human Remains, Burial Grounds, and Sacred Places: Panel Discussion," *Wicazo Sa Review* Vol. 19, No. 2, Colonization/Decolonization (Autumn 2004): pp. 169–83.

before I ever got to know him. I see myself walking alone up to that monument on the hill with my tobacco in hand, wind blowing over me, age twenty-two to thirty-five, all the changes in weight, experience, and self, going to pray at that grave, which it turns out Grandpa Sammy was completely instrumental in divining the placement of. His mystery, medicine, and life, folding into me from a young age; his emanations finding me, his legacy sealing the bond. I always get teary when I really start to feel his spirit. One time he told me that the love he carries for the People and the love I carry for the People are the same, and that's why we can work so closely and well together. I feel the tears in my chest and take a breath; no witnesses, but in this work there seldom are.

A top-hatted metalhead chats with the hardened barista and I reread the passage, chuckle that the single mention of Sammy that I can find online just so happens to speak directly to these very personal parts of my life. I shake my head at the weirdness of how it took me so long to do the most obvious thing that everyone does nowadays when they want to learn more about something or someone, to look him up online. Another piece of Grandpa Sammy stitched into the patchwork of my spirit; more of his essence accrued in my body; another demonstration of Yoda's real, active powers. I wonder what Denny's going to think about this. I believe he knew about me when he was still alive, of the work his grandson and I were coming to do; Medicine Men on his level operate in ways far beyond what most of us can imagine. It's a comfort to the part of me that knows my destiny. I wish I had a cigarette. I imagine Sammy seeing those little kids coming to him in their old-time clothes, that old man telling him where to rebury the remains, him feeling and knowing the profound manifestations of healing and relief and harmony that will come to the descendants involved once all are properly put to rest in the earth again. I imagine Sammy on his way to wherever he was going to sleep that night, thinking of the immense, unconscionable atrocities that had been done to our People, and then all the ways we were still blood-empowered to use our gifts to set things right. I see the look in his eyes as he thinks about these things and take another drink of my coffee.

Some loud, drunk tourists come stumbling in, drinks in hand, trying to balance their respect for the over-it locals with their unleashed desire to get what they've come for. I look at the thoughts in their eyes, check my phone for anything from Aislinn—nothing—and then reconnect with Sammy and remember this dream I had in Seattle. In the dream I was lying on a couch watching this documentary about these Medicine Men, and a full third of it was all about Grandpa Sammy, composed of interviews with contemporaries and other Medicine Men who shared generously about the man they knew. I watched one old guy, standing outside as it began to get dark behind him, who said, "He was always getting grief, getting criticized by people, even by his family. But Sammy had seen thousands and thousands of years into the future, and he carried that ultimate vision in his heart, calibrating his every thought, word, and action toward the service of that vision, down to the smallest little thing. People didn't understand him and so they judged him, but they didn't know what he lived with."

I woke up from that dream wrapped in a blanket of words from the ancestors, my forever-lonesome self covered by the dream-received comfort and teachings of all the spirits who were helping me to make the most of my life, who were showing me how medicine could be made wherever I went. I rolled out of my back bedroom, grabbed my cigarettes, and went outside to our front steps to think about the dream.

For the nourishment it gave my heart and imagination, I interpreted it literally. No such documentary actually existed, but I imagined Sammy really going on a visionary tour of our People's lives thousands of years into the future, receiving into the bundle of his body and spirit a first-hand sacred knowledge-map of what was to come, what was to remain, what was going to be intact, of how he was to use his life and medicine to work in tandem with the spirits to do his part in engineering the realization of that already-secured reality. Some of the things that happened to Sammy and that he experienced are both too unbelievable and family-owned to ever be put into words on a page, but knowing of some of them, I can say that what this old man shared with me in that dream was very much within the realm of possibility. I pictured Sammy spending weeks and weeks among the People in that far-off time, applying everything in his specially-trained consciousness to the study of their existence, culture, enlightenment, and ways of being with the Earth and Cosmos, ingesting it all so that he would know and have and be able to figure out the medicine that was needed by all the different storylines back in the present. I imagined the Creator granting such a spiritual experience to an old grandpa in North Dakota, whose time was limited but whose legacy would be without end. I smoked my cigarette and wondered at the things Sammy must've known, at the work he must've woken up to everyday. I blew my smoke out into the night and saw him beholding with all his Elder's humanity the reality of how our People had successfully survived everything, how vibrant we still were, how the calamity of colonization had left its mark but was also mostly gone, like some faint ghost drifting by in the wind. I reflected on my dream and felt nothing but pure hope.

My phone goes off and I see that Aislinn isn't giving a tour tonight, that she's going to be biking over from Royal Street pretty soon. I put all my stuff back into my bag and finish my coffee. I know that Sammy will be with me until the end and that's a powerful thing to know. We've come here to work on some things that might not see their flowering or completion for a hundred or maybe even a thousand years, and that's okay; it's all about the company we keep while we're here. I laugh and feel some of the other dreams I've had of Sammy surfacing in my chest, like '70s underground-cartoon fish all poking their noses at the inside of my sweaty shirt, their smells wafting out to join the rich aromas of the Quarter like Indian secrets that'll surely find the right audience someday. Aislinn and I will probably bike over to the Mississippi and sit on the stone steps with the smattering of others who're there, feel some of that grand evening peace before we jump back into the jagged, chomping maw of the city (it's one of my favorite things to do here because the river is always ready to throw its arm over your shoulder and remind you of what's really up). I bus my table and go outside to unlock and retrieve my bike.

A horse and carriage clip-clops by and things feel like they're getting tighter, a little more unruly, like the Quarter's stomach is beginning to bulge and the hard spirits are kicking in. I wheel away from my column to the other side of Cafe Envie where I know I'll be seeing Aislinn in just a couple of minutes. I wonder what she'll think about my Grandpa Sam-my Google discovery; she's incredibly sensitive and has also dreamed of him and feels him when he's around. I post up and look down the street in front of me, feel glad that I've sworn off drinking again since I moved here so that I can avoid that piece of the New Orleans underworld, so that I can spare myself that grief as I've already got grief enough as an on-the-mend Indian. I think about asking the quiet young man wearing only one shoe at the nearby table for a cigarette but then think better of it and just keep waiting. My phone dings, "On my way!"

I see her peddling toward me, going fast like she's so ready to see me and get the hell out of here, her front basket full and shaking with stuff. She's beautiful. Waving. That thing we all want growing ever closer. Ever find the person you want to ride your bike off into the sunset with? That's her. I wave back. What if decades from now we're still together? What if next year? I bike toward her, lining up with her, intentionally putting myself on a collision course.

"Aislinn!" I yell, catching looks. "Aislinn!" Like our reunion is the big point of it all tonight. "Hurry up! Let's get out of here!" She smiles, laughs, vigorously nods. And then we both quit messing around and really, really start peddling.

137 YEARS LATER

THIS IS A DREAM:

I'm hopping on a train and finding my way to this Medicine Man's ranch. I'm not the only one. Via a couple other scenes of travel, I gather that there are a number of people heading his way, almost like for a little gathering.

The tracks rumble beneath us. We're not passengers, we're train-hoppers. The hot day blasts across everything. And I begin to hear this Medicine Man's voice, speaking through all of space, coming from everywhere.

"The Story is in the Seed!" he says very emphatically.

I feel very happy in my heart that I'm on my way to his place.

He says it again; a message rippling through the whole environment.

"The Story is in the Seed!"

We get to his place out in the desert, and I hear him say it one last time; the main thing he wants me to know, to remember.

"The Story is in the Seed!"

And then I wake up.

And suddenly I had a life I never imagined would really be mine.

I lived in the Central District in Seattle with my hometown blood-brother Clark and our roommate Joe, two queer party animals and a sober Indian in a three-bedroom apartment. Our landlord intentionally kept our rent low and affordable as his way of fighting the good fight. One time a bartender who was sleeping on our couch told me, "You've found the unicorn. There's no other apartment like this in downtown Seattle."

I had no bed in my bedroom. I just laid on a couple of blankets and watched stuff on my laptop, vibrated in the very present mythological energy of the city. I had a box of books I'd brought with me, my worn-out clothes, and my tub of sacred stuff, which included a little red cloth pouch of ancestral Ponca corn that my friend Barbara had given to me on my way out of Nebraska. I'd never planted anything before in my life, but then again that was the ultimate promise of Seattle: to experience some things that I never had before in my life.

It was one of those semi-rare moments in the apartment when I had the place to myself. Joe was off managing the kitchen at his dive hipster taco pub and Clark was doing his day job accountant thing. It was time. I grabbed the pouch of seeds, some tobacco, left my humble bedroom, took an immediate left into Joe's messy-like-an-alcoholic-Swampthing's bedroom, stepped around all his stuff, and then climbed through the designated backdoor that was his bedroom window and went on down the cinderblock steps out into our prodigious backyard.

I held the seeds and tobacco in my hand.

Native life was all about keeping the ways alive, and thereby keeping all the intricate layers of our identity alive too.

Ponca life was all about growing the Ponca existence forward so that it would be there for all the future Ponca.

I walked to the garden, trying to feel all the sacred implications of what I was about to do.

In 2014, our sacred Ponca corn was planted and grown in our Nebraska homelands for the first time in 137 years. The last time we'd planted it as a tribe was the summer we were forcibly marched down to Oklahoma by the US Government on our Trail of Tears. The corn was left standing, unharvested, along with everything else we were made to abandon.

The corn came back to us.

Amos Hinton, then agriculture director of the Ponca Tribe of Oklahoma, wanting for our People to be able to eat and be nourished by our ancestral foods again, tracked our corn down via three sources: a Pawnee woman working to locate corn varieties original to Oklahoma tribes, a farmer who'd been growing corn from that crop we'd left behind, and a Lakota family who'd also been doing the same.

My friend Barbara was there when they planted the corn in 2014 (I'd read about the planting in the newspaper at my gas station) and when I visited her on my way to Seattle, she gave me that little pouch of seeds. At the time, Barbara was doing Ponca language work for the tribe, pouring her efforts into that crucial core area. I'm pretty sure I had no idea what I was really receiving.

What does it mean for our corn to come back to us?

In the articles covering the return of our corn, Hinton is quoted as saying, "In our Creation Story the Creator gave us three original gifts: red corn, a dog, and a bow."

What does it mean for all of us Ponca today to be able to hold in our hands one of the original gifts that the Creator gave to us?

What does it mean?

Another stellar feature of our Seattle apartment was its very large, fenced-in backyard. By the time I'd moved in, Joe and Clark had had a huge garden going for seven consecutive summers and it was a bona fide plant miracle-space/labor-of-love/well-tended god of the best sort. (Clark grew over ten kinds of peppers alone; one time he came home and told me that he'd gotten a new tattoo; asking me if I'd like to see it, I said yes, and he lifted up his shirt to reveal a beautiful, long, red, hot pepper on his ribcage.) I'd always respected Mother Earth, loved her in an easy, natural way, but as a creature my main domains were libraries, coffee shops, my apartment, and downtown Lincoln. It was cool that we had a garden, but I was about as far away from being any kind of initiated gardener as you could be, you know?

I didn't exactly know the proper way to plant my People's corn, but I was a Sundancer and did know how to pray, so I walked up to where there were already about a hundred things planted and stood where Joe had left me a big strip of rich black soil for my corn; not having any instructions in my mind but full of feelings that *seemed* instructional and very much of the seeds in my hand. I thought of my Elders, thought, *Humility is its own special ingredient.*

I looked down at the colorful garden and opened up the pouch that Barbara had given me, pouring a few of the truly magical seeds into my palm, going one step at a time. I wasn't sure of how many to plant, so I just portioned off seven of them, as that was always a good number, and then I put the rest back into the pouch. I had my tobacco. I had some songs. I probably should've taken off my shoes but didn't. I walked to the top of my soil strip and got down on my knees, peered into the space I was working with, rested there for a second. I was sure my Ponca ancestors were there in the garden with me.

Totally a beginner but clear about what I was doing, I prayed and pushed each of the little seeds a couple inches down into the ground, making almost like a constellation layout, putting some tobacco down with each one, hoping they would take and sprout and grow—whatever that meant. It didn't take long. It felt good to do it, like I was a schoolkid following up on some sacred business. I planted all seven seeds and then rose up and brushed off my knees. Now it was time to sing.

Hot, guided by my ancestors, my brother Clark—my only friend in that whole big new city—I closed my eyes and began singing to my corn.

In my early twenties, I had a falling out with a good older work-friend when, after an unexpectedly heated exchange, he said to me, "We won the war. You lost. Now get over it."

That was his stance when it came to what had happened with us Indians. And it's actually the unexamined thought a lot of Americans have about us.

So many thoughts creating ignorant blindness where there should actually be natural, powerful vision.

Another misguided thought is that we Indians—actually, let me get very specific—we Ponca have lost all our culture, or most of it anyway. The mountain of it was obliterated and now there are just a couple of pitiful pebbles. America destroyed us, assimilated us, boarding-schooled us, stomped us to nothing, turned us into so many more lost nameless consumerist Americans. America won the war.

We had our last Ponca Sundance in 1908.

We haven't had a traditional Medicine Man in almost a century.

There are no fluent speakers among us Northern Ponca.

We have no bundles left.

A grim picture, for sure.

When I first got active and into learning about our People I kind of believed it: what did we actually have left?

Twenty years later and the spirits have packed me full of a completely different understanding.

The mountain was never obliterated, just a part of it.

We're not walking around with nothing; we're walking around with complete worlds nesting inside us.

If I were to obliterate anything, it'd be this thought that says we don't have anything left but the poor little bit that's at the bottom of the bucket.

The reality is that there is more than enough Ponca culture left to regrow all of what we had and then some. Seriously.

It's hard to believe sometimes, but it's true.

That beautiful mountain that our ancestors lived on and loved so much is still right there: living, breathing, and talking to us in this very moment.

It was crazy.

I'd sweat once or twice (or more) a month for thirteen years, crawling in there to pray and learn just like my ancestors did, and then when I moved to Seattle I suddenly went a solid year without a sweat. My grandma died and I had no way to really get back for her funeral. Seattle was a blast, but my loneliness hadn't entirely lost track of me. Now I didn't even have the comfort of my People to help me out when I needed it. I thought about all of this while walking home from Safeway, where I worked as a cashier. It was past five o'clock and I had no plans again. I lit a cigarette and comforted myself, walking up and down those famous hills.

I made it to our block and waved to the people inside of Katy's Café, passed the qigong studio, the subterranean pirate radio station, the squatting stone camel with the visible genitals, looked for the sweet dreadlocked blonde who owned the kombucha shop, checked out what Central Cinema was playing, and then arrived home. But, instead of going in, I went around the side of our building to check on my corn.

Instantly, I just felt so happy.

Standing there and having another cigarette because what the hell, I grinned like someone who'd just received a sweet handwritten letter from the spirits, seeing six little green plants enjoying their first inch of life above ground. I wondered: was I the first Ponca to ever grow corn in Seattle? I heard whisperings from everything my Ponca soul ever wanted to be close to. They looked like fibrous origami, perfect residents in our glorious grunge rock garden.

I admired them and smoked. *We're with you. We're not just in the past, we're unfurling in the freshest moments of the present too. Your prayers are making up the books the next Ponca will be reading in the future. We're geniuses at keeping things Indigenous. Every strange brushstroke is essential for the finished painting. We were here even before the pipe. We travel well together. The more you grow us, the more we'll grow you. Can you hear the song we're singing for you?*

Six out of seven wasn't bad as far as I was concerned. I grew up in a trailer with a rolling field of GMO corn standing thick behind us every summer and now I was a thirty-five-year-old Ponca growing six stalks of ancestral corn in our stoner's fairy tale backyard garden; a mysterious storyteller's poetry was tying everything together everywhere. Maybe I didn't know what I was getting myself into, like in a good way. I loved my little sprouting corn plants, LOVED THEM. Who knew what they could become? I let my eyes rest on them and thought so strongly of home that it was like I was really somehow there.

Our Ponca culture was never just a finite, material thing given to the People long ago to grip onto, fearfully worrying that if it was ever lost or misplaced that'd mean that it was gone forever.

Our Ponca culture has always been a mysterious, layered, encompassing thing that cyclically replenishes itself through the generations, that's actually inexhaustible, adaptable, luminously alive in an immeasurable number of beautiful manifestations.

We can pray.

We can fast.

We can dream.

We can collaborate with our ancestors every day and work with them on this grand project of regenerating our sacred culture in these unique times.

We can make a spirit-plate.

We can make offerings to the rivers, plants, hills, lakes, stars, animals, spirits, trees, fish, butterflies, and such, all the same ones that our ancestors had long-running relationships with up in Niobrara; these relatives have not forgotten us, they're ready to give and share.

If we're not around Niobrara, we can make offerings to all the similar life around us like our ancestors did and root ourselves down into the same Indigenous intelligence and style of being that they were so reverently steeped in.

We can HANG OUT WITH OTHER INDIANS.

We can TALK TO OLD PEOPLE.

We can learn from our relatives of other tribes.

We are building up our tribal infrastructure so that we may receive sacred things that are already on their way, including things we've lost and also things not yet imagined.

We can grow corn.

We can speak words that literally ran through the minds and mouths of our People for thousands of years.

We can sweat.

We can Sundance.

We can carry a pipe.

Endless are the ways we Ponca can proudly embody and radiate our essence.

This is the thing to never forget.

If you're Ponca, then you've already won half the battle.

Pray, talk to your ancestors, and see what happens.

Pretty soon people were going to start showing up for one of our backyard bonfires; congregating, laughing, smoking, drinking, telling stories, enjoying themselves late into the night. Maybe some of our lovely neighbors would join us, maybe Clark would throw another old Christmas tree into the fire, and we'd all stand back in gleeful awe as the wild blast of light suddenly illuminated everything. Chances were something Seattle-style magical would happen.

But for now, I was alone, with the backyard and garden all to myself. So, I made my way over to my corn, knowing there were mysteries to be related to in the stalks and flesh of them.

I stood there in my cargo shorts and admired them: they were getting to be almost as tall as I was, and there were even some small ears beginning to bud out from them. It was like I'd been given a sacred riddle from the kindest grandpa spirit and the only bit of helpful advice he'd passed along was, "If you stare at it long enough, you'll get it." You got what was waiting for you through daily contemplation and doing it long enough. The garden was a fantastic teeming metropolis of vines, vegetables, and leaves, with my corn as a long earthy summer yawn, lightning carefully wrapped in plant tissue, so many Native ballerinas happily smiling up at the sky.

I stared at my corn and began to slip into a very real, mystical, altered state. Another dimension of what the corn really was opened up to me and I silently fell deeper and deeper into my experience of it. I looked at the long leaves, all the warm overspilling mass of these sacred Ponca corn plants, and I almost tearfully saw how they were the souls of my ancestors incarnate. The corn smoked and smoldered with the bodies, forms, images, and consciousness of my ancestors, steamed with their presence to the point that I understood the corn as both communicator of them and actually secretly made up of them. Like the corn wasn't actually composed of cells, but of my actual Ponca ancestors themselves!

I stared and stared and knew I was experiencing something few would understand, but also something that every Ponca who grew their corn was on some level built to understand. This planted Ponca corn was a direct, powerful portal into the timeless source-realm from which all Ponca—past, present, and future—were fundamentally linked to and came from. I wasn't standing in front of just some corn in my backyard, I was standing with Ponca ancestors who could engulf me with their presence and hand me things precious beyond my imagining. I understood what was happening as it was happening. This was what the reappearance of our Ponca corn had to offer to our tribe and to every tribal member with all their grief and heart's longing.

I swayed in the wind of the Creator and experienced my corn, thunderstruck by its sacred mysteries and medicine.

Seven Thoughts about Corn and Indians from My Brother Denny

1. Turtle Islanders remember that in The First Age a woman sat in the sky, grinding out corn that fell to the earth.
2. We fucking ate that corn.
3. In comparison to rice and wheat, what corn was before Turtle Islanders put their hands on it resembles nothing it does today nor does it have the nutrients of today—that means there was no reason to work with it.

4. Turtle Islanders remember that Corn Woman in the sky taught us what to do with the grass that corn began as.
5. Turtle Islanders have stories that Corn Woman was old, and they have stories that Corn Woman was young.
6. Turtle Islanders remember a different history of our sky, a different arrangement of our solar system.
7. Venus is known by many names on Turtle Island, and they reflect different ways it moved, different colors and appearances, different things it did, and a much closer location to our earth.

And then just like that I was in love.

Aislinn and I met at a ceremony in Louisiana, became pen pals (she asked me, "Do you wanna be pen pals?"), kindled the beginning of something more in Kauai, and then she came to Seattle, with her initial week-long visit turning into her moving in with Clark and Joe and me for a couple months. I wasn't sure if my life had ever been so thoroughly saturated by love and beauty. She'd go and busk in Pike Place Market, writing poems for strangers on her typewriter while I cashiered at Safeway, and then we'd meet up when I got off work. This was our routine for week after week after week. I waited for her in Joe's bedroom by his backyard window door. It was time to harvest maybe one or two of the biggest ears of my corn.

"Are you ready?" she asked, excited for me, completely sensitive to the sacredness of what was growing in our garden.

I smiled and nodded. "Let's go look at the corn."

We both climbed through the open window and hopped down the cinderblock steps, eyeing our artistic and messy backyard, then hand in hand walked over to my robust and shining corn, now well over six feet tall. Aislinn slipped off her sandals, let her bare feet greet the edge of our wild, wondrous garden. I squeezed her hand, so infinitely happy to have someone to share all this with, and partially floated into the golden auras of my lovely plants.

"They look like they're ready," she said. "Especially those two big ones."

I agreed, saying, "Those are the two my untrained eyes see as well."

There were about five good ears altogether and two more latecomers that surely still had a chance. It'd been a joy and a delight and a pleasure to watch my plants produce their corn, the seeds I'd need to do this again next summer, their smooth edible ears. They were my friends, my Elders, my ancestors, my personal portal into the Ponca source-realm in the spirit world, and now it was time to follow them forward into the next part of our friendly, ancient dance.

"Do you need to pray first?" Aislinn asked.

"I think I'll talk to them while I do it, I guess," I replied.

I stepped into the garden, went up to the stalk with the largest ear, expressed my gratitude, my love, told them how thankful I was for everything, this moment, Aislinn, the gift of seeds from Barbara, the huge ear of corn, Seattle, the ineffable journey I was on as a Ponca poet from Nebraska; and then I took the tender ear in my hand and slowly cracked it free, pulling it off. I felt like I was holding one of the original bundles of my People. It was hefty and light at the same time. A piece of what I held immediately passed into my remembering heart, there to stay forever as a facet of my destiny. I cradled it in my arms and smiled so big you would've thought I'd just been given the best news of my life.

I turned to Aislinn and showed her my corn, practically raised it up to her. She mirrored back pure joy, was half lost in a radiance that was coming from all directions, that I myself was half-gone in too.

Smiling and praying, I moved on to carefully harvesting the next one.

Before I left Lincoln I had this dream:

I was lying on the bed in the small trailer I grew up in. I was my adult self, but I was in the bedroom I'd had when I was a teenager.

I lay there and then I began to hear Crow Dog speaking to me from the little crack beneath the closed door. Just his voice, talking to me.

He said, "Nephew, you've been looking for the Ponca Elders to teach you about the culture, but you're not going to find them."

It was true. I wanted to meet those Ponca Elders who could teach me all the stuff; like some monk before the invention of the printing press who wanted to meet all the right monks who had all the Ponca books so that I could hand copy them all and have their full resource as a part of my own library.

He went on, just his voice coming from that crack under the door.

"But that's okay. Because what you're looking for in them the spirits have grown in you. Their substance is in you."

I tried to comprehend what he was saying and then I woke up.

Crow Dog had been coming to me in dreams about every six months or so since I'd met him, over ten years ago. I always paid close attention to what he had to say, even if I didn't always follow up on it.

I felt like he was saying this very specific thing was coming to an end as I was moving to Seattle, a thing he expressed so perfectly: that particular search was over.

Maybe the dream will be viewed as controversial; it's easy for me to imagine people's reactions and responses. There are obviously plenty of Ponca Elders still around, plenty of books, so to speak, to seek out and hand copy so that they're not lost.

How do dreamworld Medicine Men understand the substance that's found in an Elder?

I've always understood him to mean that what the spirits had been growing in me for the last twenty years was now entirely capable of empowering me to do all the things I was set to do next.

Be confident and move forward, is what I heard.

Give up your looking and trust in what you've been given.

Aislinn took a couple pictures of me posing with the two enormous ears of corn that I'd picked; with me smiling and looking upwards like some first-time farmer overflowing with happiness, holding them in my arms like the miraculous children that they were. Everything that was happening at this point felt like another gorgeously crafted chapter in our passionate, multidimensional romance, including harvesting the undeniably sacred world-building superstar of my sweet corn. After we took our pictures, we climbed through Joe's bedroom window and went back inside.

We could hear that both Clark and Joe were home, convening in the kitchen where we all crossed paths and caught up and often feasted before retiring to our different bedrooms. We carried the corn out to the kitchen, to say hello and show them the beautiful ears.

"Holy guacamole!" Joe yelled, thrift store t-shirt extra tight over his life-lover's belly. "Your corn!"

Clark sat on a kitchen chair with a look in his eyes like he'd just caught a glimpse of the world's rarest whale on his long walk home from work. "Look at those babies," he said.

I cocked my head, grinning. "Us or the corn?"

"All of you," he laughed.

"Aren't they perfect?" Aislinn asked.

I'd come to the apartment as the struggling younger Midwestern friend, and Clark and Joe had been my loud and tireless cheerleaders, wanting for me to have the life of my dreams in the city that Clark regularly and sincerely called "the greatest city on Earth." In their eyes, every successful endeavor deserved some serious celebration; it was all once faraway happiness now righteously inhaled/ingested/enjoyed. They loved on my corn as much as they loved on me; I just tried to come out of my shell so that I could receive it.

"Can we boil it and eat it like sweet corn then?" Joe asked. "Can we eat it tonight?"

"My friend Barbara who gave me the seeds must've been feeling us while we were out there. She sent me a text and I think it's about the corn," I said. "Let me read it real quick." I stood there reading her texts while everyone else got drinks and put some music on and then I shared what she'd said. "Actually, I guess you don't eat it like sweet corn. I didn't even know that. She says you dry it out and grind it up and then make stuff from it. She also said to save the leaves from the ears to make like traditional cigarettes out of them."

"Oh," Joe said. "No corn dripping with butter tonight then."

We all looked at each other, pausing and processing, visions running through us like some illuminated corn versions of the *Where the Wild Things Are* creatures, oozing with good life vibes all around.

"Maybe we should all eat some raw anyway, just a bit, to symbolically celebrate your corn's success," Joe said, saying what sounded like an excellent idea right away.

I looked at Clark and he shrugged affirmatively. "Let's do it," I said, holding up the biggest ear. "Should I go first?"

They all looked at me and I carefully peeled back the corn some, clearing its finer silks, exposing about half of it, and then, because it felt right, I took a bite. It tasted good. It tasted all right. This moment we were all having with the corn was just like so many other moments in the apartment: it was delicious, bright, and full.

I handed the ear to Aislinn and she held it and eyed it with love. She looked at me, I nodded, and then she took her bite. Then Joe went. And then Clark went. We all chewed and talked and commented on its tastiness, its sweetness.

"This is corn from Nebraska before Nebraska was Nebraska," Clark said, savoring it in his way. "I fucking love it."

My grandson and I drove my daughter's truck out to the Ponca Sundance grounds, drinking cold drinks and feeling the early summer heat coming through the open windows. I'd always hoped I'd live long enough to have good times with my grandkids like my grandpa had had with me and now, thank the Creator, I was.

We cruised into some of that old Ponca backcountry and talked about the trees, cartoons, school, and the spirits too, which all Indians liked to hear about, as every story told about the spirits vibrates with the cultural energy of the old times, the times when such energy was defining and everywhere.

It didn't take long, but soon we were there at the grounds; nobody was around but the place was far from empty, last year's tree standing tall, the arbor made of wood and nails and supernatural light. I would never forget what it felt like on that day when so many Ponca got to place their hands on the tree during that first Ponca Sundance that we'd had in over a hundred years, in over five or six generations. And here we were now having one every summer, proudly and beautifully so.

"Should we go make an offering at the tree?" I asked my grandson, seeing my and so many other faces inside of his. He seemed excited; it was a good sign that he liked to do what Grandpa liked to do, at least I thought so.

I took out my little pouch, opened it, and told him, "This is from the Ponca corn we grew. Take three kernels. We're going to offer them to the tree, thank that warrior who's standing there."

He took three purple-red kernels with his little brown hand and then so did I.

We got out of the truck.

"Think you can sing a song for us after we're done praying?" I asked.

"Yeah," he nodded.

We started walking on that holy earth toward the tree.

"Good. We're set then," I said. "Cause the spirits always like it when the young people sing."

Aislinn was in the shower, getting ready (I was going to surprise her by taking her to a true sacred site that was right in Seattle: Bruce Lee's grave), and I was sitting at our kitchen table, drinking a kombucha, looking at our neighbor's neat house, and then I drifted over to the corn that was drying and hanging in our window. They were like four long organic jewels, held up by the ropes of their braided leaves; a wonderful part of our found art/epicurean's cartoon kitchen.

I'd been given seeds, I planted them, I saw them through to their harvest, and now I had what I needed to do it all over again next year drying out above my head. Such are the dreams we are all made for. Such are the everyday, earth-grown dreams we are all here for.

I looked at the corn and let my consciousness spiral outwards until I was standing with the Corn Mother Herself when She was first instructing our People in how to work with Her and Her seeds and plants, until I was spiritually fanned out into all of the Ponca and Indians and souls who would ever work with Her, until I was in over a thousand different ceremonies that were all lovingly dedicated to Her, until I was gone into the Corn Mother's own origins, until I was surging in all the sacred reasons and purposes for which She grew among us poetry-filled two-leggeds; and then I came back and just felt Her as I looked at Her hanging in the window.

I didn't tell anyone, but I felt like no fool for believing in the ultimate inevitability of all the dreams I carried for my People; my secret was that I'd already been shown that such healed, enlightened, Indigenous-centered realities were coming: like the return of our corn after 137 years, these other spirits, ceremonies, and realities were coming back too.

I heard the shower stop and loved my corn, loved where I'd come from, loved my brother Clark, loved Aislinn, loved my skin and bones and soul and life I'd been given; loved it all until I was the seed I was meant to be, the seed I'd always been, and then I loved everything I saw in that moment too.

I looked at my corn and waited for Aislinn, bubbling over at the kitchen table. "Next year it's me and you," I said to my corn. "Next year it's me and you and hopefully Aislinn too!"

VISITING THE HOMELANDS

SUNDANCE DONE, OUR gear in our car (my brother's actually; borrowed), we drove across Santee, flying through the burning morning. Forty-one, I was a slab of happiness and contentment, cooked deep brown. Aislinn, her third year at our Sundance behind her, was comfortable, knew everybody, told me how she felt like she really belonged there, which was part of a very real journey for her as on some days she was the only white person there. What a trip it had been. The verdant earth turned and slipped on by us.

"I'm so tired, but I at least want to do a drive-by of the powwow grounds and cemetery," I said, watching the road. "We can't be this close and not cruise by. It's a howling must."

"We've got time," said Aislinn. "Today's only goal is to get back to your brother's. No rush."

We drove and talked, launched our awareness into the nearby Missouri River, brushed against those painterly bluffs, unraveled Sundance stories, compared notes, sighed, laughed, and smiled. My People's homelands enveloped us and talked to our prayerful minds. Our Sundance on Santee was maybe a half hour tops from our Ponca powwow grounds/buffalo pasture/cemetery, from that big, concentrated essence of our tribe's being. I missed being just a couple hour drive away from it all; I missed having that relatively easy access to everything I kept returning back to, to know myself and to know my People. Now that we were living on the Oregon Coast, we were lucky to make it back about once a year.

We both understood the preciousness of these Nebraska trips. We both understood that I wouldn't have been whole without them.

We slowed down and breezed through the small town of Niobrara, and I told Aislinn the story of how I'd gotten pulled over for speeding one time way past dark after we'd finally gotten our tree up, wearing only my swim trunks and having forgotten my wallet, trying to get one last shower in before we began dancing the following morning.

"What happened?"

"I prayed and told the officer what I was doing and why I didn't have my wallet on me. I was so nervous. He could've taken me in and that would've been it for me that year, no Sundance, not for me. But he either must've been familiar with the Sundance or he just could feel the utter sincerity of my energy, because he let me go, just told me to slow down and make sure I had my wallet on me next time. Ugh, that was such a close call."

"The spirits were with you that night."

"They must've been. Holy smokes."

We crossed my People's river, the Niobrara, and then we crossed another and took the turn to the powwow grounds. How many times had I made that turn in my life? How many times had my dad? It's such a beautiful thing to have done something a million times when you're an Indian and you're on your People's land. In those instances, those situations, even if it's just making a turn on an old gravel road, you almost feel like nothing was ever really taken from you at all; so full and in the soul-essence of your People you can be. I winked at the dinged-up powwow road sign and could've sworn that it winked right back.

A few minutes later and we were upon it: the modernized, circular arbor, our agency building, our fleshed-out campgrounds so full of family memories, and all the new stuff too—education trail, Chief Standing Bear statue—that I hadn't really checked out yet. All of it rising up as we approached it like some physical expression of all the songs the ancestors have been singing for us since we staggered our way through and out of the hell of the last century. Homecoming. Arena lights. Sweats late at night. All three Cliffs camped out together. An energy beam of Spirit hit me, and I thanked the Creator for my life and for getting to be Ponca.

"Look! That's Dan Sasuweh's sculpture. You know the guy who wrote that Ponca ghost story book? He created that, and maybe about five more of them too, all based on traditional Ponca stories."

We pulled into the grounds, which I proudly felt like were mine, because they kind of were since they belonged to all Ponca, and immediately parked by Dan's big copper monkey statue that was planted right in front of our agency building. The monkey was dressed in regalia and emerging from a square black panel, kind of reminiscent of Han Solo frozen-imprisoned in that carbonite in *The Empire Strikes Back*—it was very artistic and cool. I wanted a picture with it for all kinds of happy, nerdy reasons. I'd just gone without food or water for four days, so give me what I want, haha!

Aislinn, supportive and camera-savvy, took several pictures of me with the grinning monkey, then of us with the monkey; a hay-colored, sun-splashed tapestry of Ponca life snug in the background behind us. It was fun. My kind of party. One day, if I was lucky and played my cards right, maybe I'd dream of that Ponca monkey spirit and get to hear a little something from him directly about what he's all about, right? We hopped back in our car and found a better place to park, by the restrooms and showers, which was perfect because we both needed to pee. "Shall we pee?" I asked. Aislinn shook her head, opened the door, and was gone.

Relieved, we walked into the stillness of the empty grounds, my center instinctively taking us toward the spot a ways away where my family camped for many, many years, memory drawing us on. We admired another copper sculpture of Dan's, peered up to see how the old area around the front part of the buffalo pasture had been modified, and then followed a little trail to the earth lodge, which was mighty and grassy and silent.

"Can we go inside?" Aislinn asked.

There was a piece of yellow tape across the entrance. "It looks solid from the outside," I said, "but maybe they don't want anyone going in."

"Too sacred?"

"Naw, probably just an insurance liability thing."

We stood at the earth lodge's entrance, kneeling down and peering in, feeling the cooler temperature inside. It was easy to imagine our ancestors in there cooking, laughing, and stargazing through the smoke hole at the top.

Aislinn, the rebel of the two of us, asked, "Should we go in anyway?"

I felt some eyes on us but couldn't be sure if they were of this world or the other.

"Maybe next time," I answered. "Let's keep walking."

We went along and read some of the educational placards, learned about our beloved Ponca corn from one, talked about how much Aislinn's dad would enjoy what we were learning from the trail, and took pictures to text to him later. We lamented the vanishing of the pond and stream that used to be near our campsite but was now just a thick, vacant pit; its horned underwater monster moved on to other waters. We gave a big gold star for serious excellence to a shade structure whose roof was all vibrant yellow prairie grasses shaking their hips in the wind. We really liked what we were feeling, appreciated how what had been created could really communicate something of our Ponca soul into the folks who visited us, could gift them with a strand of our luminosity that would potentially last a lifetime.

"A part of me wishes it had stayed wild and uncultivated, just raw, bare land like how it was when I was a kid," I said, looking out at pieces of other projects in the nearby field. "But I guess this is growing on me. I can see what we're trying to do. I can see the thought behind it."

"I hope we can make it back for the powwow," Aislinn said, taking a drink from her water bottle.

"I do too. You should see what this place looks like when everything's in full swing. It's like a big Ponca family reunion. It's awesome."

She handed me the water bottle, looked around and said, "I bet it is."

Feeling the long drive ahead of us and, honestly, a little itchy to get going, I stopped us short from going too much further and turned us back around to head to our overstuffed car. It was bittersweet. I wasn't ready to leave, but my energy was low, my gas tank not much more than fumes. Were these the decisions we had to make peace with as adults? Just take comfort in how alive it was inside of you and be okay with saying goodbye early? We got back to our ride, and I paused to soak it up and then, from a row of small trailers south of us, I heard, "Clifford! Clifford! Is that you?"

We looked toward a dark-haired woman who was coming our way and immediately I recognized her from her online profile picture.

"Stacy?" I yelled.

"Who's that?" Aislinn asked.

"It's Stacy Larvie. Our dads grew up together. We were messaging about meeting up while I was here, but I just couldn't make it happen with our schedules."

Stacy approached with open arms and we hugged.

"Wow," she said. "You walk just like your dad."

The three of us sat on a picnic table in front of a newer trailer where Stacy said she and her teenage son were staying for the weekend, half for work-related reasons (Stacy was our Tribal Historic Preservation Officer), and half just to enjoy the beauty of where we were. She was smart, present, tired-seeming, had big, dark eyes, and a passion in her person that was refreshing and relatable.

"I'm so glad you saw me," I told her, catching a second wind. "I'm so glad we decided to cruise through. I think we must've met as kids, but I don't remember. I love the songs you share online. You have a beautiful voice. This is cool."

Aislinn couldn't help herself, "I think this was meant to happen. This is totally the ancestors."

And then Stacy, "We have so much to talk about."

Maybe I'm getting a little ahead of myself but the conversation flowed, flooding between the three of us, rushing and electric and somersaulting, zipping about like spirit-catfish that were bigger than we were and faster than lightning; the earth around us perspired like an old man in the sweat on the verge of having a vision (haha). I actually can't remember the last time I'd talked with a fellow Ponca my age—and that's on me—about so many different casual and deep Ponca-specific things that were alive in my own mind and big-picture thinking. We passed through the gateway of our dads and long-ago family memories, and then we were joyously chatterboxing away, reflecting, digging into tribal history, politics, public happenings, spirituality, yesterday's business, our visions for the future, camping stories, family jokes, everything. Too much to really share here but I will share some because sharing some is what it's all about.

"I don't know if most people grasp how powerful it was for us to get Chief Standing Bear's tomahawk-pipe back," Stacy said, flipping the page on things. "That's a relic, a powerful medicine object for our tribe."

Just a month earlier, Chief Standing Bear's tomahawk-pipe was returned to us from the Peabody Museum of Archaeology and Ethnology of Harvard University, because they recognized it was time to return the culturally significant Native items they had in their possession. Stacy was intimately involved with this repatriation, appearing in many of the photos that were making the rounds online in connection with the story.

"I don't like to say the word artifact," she continued. "They're not artifacts. They're living, breathing pieces of our People's being. That was difficult for me. I got a lot of flack and criticism for handling it and driving it back across the country to Nebraska. They say women aren't supposed to touch such things. It's not our way. But that's where I found myself, in the position where it was my responsibility to make sure our grandpa's pipe got home, and there wasn't a man standing there to do it, but there was me. My dad and uncles raised me like a boy, teaching and sharing our Ponca ways with me; I believe they were raising me to do the things I'm doing now, that are my life now. As a tribe we're not at a place where we can do everything like we used to. We're rebuilding, so we have to do what we can with what we have, to get to where we're regenerated enough that we have the right, qualified people on hand to competently carry out all the roles that are required for our tribe to be healthy and functional and whole. Some will get mad, but we have to trust that our ancestors are guiding us, and they understand. It's like with the storm that uprooted all the trees in the cemetery. Have you seen that yet?"

Aislinn and I looked at each other, shook our heads. I tried to gaze up to the cemetery but couldn't exactly see what she was referring to.

"I have to look in the roots of those trees to see if there are any root-ball men there, that were put there a long time ago. There should be a man doing that, to handle them in case any are found, but there's just me. This is how these things go. I'm doing my best."

I pictured one of these old spiritually active bundles entangled in the dirt-clod-laden roots of a yanked-out tree, and then I asked her, "Have you found any yet?"

She adjusted herself on her side of the picnic table. "Not yet."

Like spirited interpretive dancers for the ancestors, we slowed down our conversation, hiccupped with laughter, shot high, hawk-dove low, doubled back for the pleasure of it and then for the necessity of it, floated along, and let about an hour plus slip by pretty easily. We drank cold pops from the fridge inside her trailer, briefly met her giant-sized, athletic son, felt the different scale of time alive in the surrounding hills just as all the generations of Ponca before us did. Stacy was sharp, creative, full of the feelings that saturated all of us. The closer you got to the center of the tribe's heart, the bigger and more expansive your own became; it was just the physics of how such things worked.

"I'm going to do my damndest to get here for the powwow next month," I said, feeling the push and longings of my own purpose. "I haven't made it since I left Nebraska six years ago, and all year I've felt like something's been telling me that I need to make it, that I need to get to the powwow somehow, so some certain things that really want to happen can happen. We spent all our money on this trip, but this year I'm really just committed to believing that it can happen."

Aislinn put her hand over mine and Stacy smiled.

"This meeting, this conversation," Stacy said, "makes me think that you are gonna be here, that this year you're going to make it to the powwow."

"I hope you're right, cousin," I said. "Naw, let me rephrase that: I believe you're right."

Overflowing and positively medicined-up from our conversation with Stacy, we waved goodbye to her and drove up the road to where the giant statue of my great-great-great grandpa Chief Standing Bear stood overlooking the powwow grounds. Several days earlier when I'd told my dad that I still hadn't seen the statue up close in person, in his own grumbly way, he told me, "I guess they put it way up high on that hill so that it's like he's watching over all of us, like he's watching over the whole tribe." Pulling into the tiny, empty parking lot and seeing him there, in his regalia with his arm outstretched in his famous courtroom pose, dignity personified in copper, I could see what he meant.

We got out of our car and the wind blew over us. The grounds below were now in miniature, like a diorama of us Ponca proudly dancing forward into the twenty-first century.

"Would you like me to take a picture of you with your grandpa?" Aislinn asked, phone in hand.

He looked toward the south, to where our cemetery was, the direction of the ancestors. I remembered a story Joe Bad had told me about how he was helping this other Medicine Man with a funeral in our Ponca cemetery, and he said he saw all these misty apparitions of olden time Ponca coming over the hill and into the cemetery toward them; he said he nodded at them and that the other, older Medicine Man told him, "They're coming to pick up their relative."

I smiled and struck a pose, felt an immense cord tying my grandpa and me together, connections that pervaded the whole of me, of my entire life.

"Yeah," I said, "try to take a good one."

Aislinn tapped away on her phone, telling me to do this, try this, look this way, shift over here, and I merged into my grandpa, hearing his moccasins walking up on the river-wet earth behind me, feeling his older hand shaking my softer one, receiving his hug, spending some time with him as a younger man, before our death-march to Oklahoma, floating in tearful reverence as he sang old Ponca songs now lost by a fire for just the two of us, meeting up with him in the barren, grief-stricken cold of that first winter south, watching his eyes as he thought about the promise he'd made to his son Bear Shield to bury him back here, back in Niobrara, where our People had been buried for untold generations, shadowing him as he walked back to Nebraska along with the handful of others, frostbitten, hungry, Bear Shield's bones with him in a burlap sack, sitting in the courtroom with him as he slayed and convinced everyone of our Indian People's humanity, a humanity which the government was systematically denying us, sitting with him in his golden years, feeling his love and wisdom coming into my heart, his story becoming my story, his laughter becoming a part of how I laugh, breathing with him as he took his last breath and prepared to join all our relatives who were across the Milky Way sitting at the drum in the next world.

"Do you think you got some good ones?" My skinnier, sunburned self was a mere cornstalk next to the stout shining tree of his statue. I kind of wished I had all day just to hang out up there with him by myself; that'd be a great way to spend a day, holy even.

"I got a lot of good ones, my love," Aislinn said. "Will you take some of me now?"

I stepped away from him and took her phone, got into a good position and began snapping photos of her with his enormous person. I prayed that not only everyone in our tribe know his story in the depths of their heart—like a myth with our immortal Ponca spirit and identity powerfully coded within it—but that everyone would also be able to hear him when he was speaking to them, guiding them, and seeding them with what they were going to need to help the tribe and to also just live a beautiful, meaningful life. I prayed and took pictures of my sweetheart and felt wonderfully happy.

"Okay, I think we got all the pictures we need," I said to Aislinn. "It's starting to get kind of late in the day. I still want to visit the cemetery, but we might have to just drive up there and not get out. I don't think we've got the time."

We both stood there looking at all the countless, lovely hills fanning out from the grounds, marveling and silent. I was always trying to get us on the road and she was always trying to linger, to do one more thing. I imagined Standing Bear joining us in our quiet reflections.

"Do you want me to drive?" she asked.

"Sure," I said.

Our cemetery was located on a steep slope just a little past the powwow grounds. It seemed like the number of people buried there had about doubled since I was a kid, but that could've just been my imagination. At one time, there was a replica of one of the tall scaffolds we sometimes used to put our People to rest on back in the old days, but it'd collapsed and was now a busted-up collection of grayed branches slowly disappearing in the grass. I had many memories that took place there, funny enough, and felt the call to go there every chance that I could. My grandpa, Cliff Senior, is not buried there, although I kind of wish that he was. I remember my grandma Barb saying, "Your grandpa didn't want to be buried there. He said nobody takes care of that place. Nobody tends to it."

"Drive to the top," I told Aislinn, my arm resting out the open window. "I guess I want to get out where my uncle Oscar is buried."

Already I could feel my need/plans to get back on the road for our two-hour drive changing. My tired time-manager was drifting away up into the clouds, like a mylar balloon let loose, and the spirits were all piling into the backseat, regal, rowdy, painted, mammoth, uncontainable, vivid, and whispering loudly.

"I feel like I've got to sing at least one song," I said, looking out at the headstones, plastic flowers, fresh dirt, blank plots. "I know I said we'd just drive through, but I wouldn't feel right if I didn't make a prayer and sing."

Aislinn drove us to the topmost part of the cemetery where there was just one cluster of graves sitting all by themselves; I grabbed my tobacco from the center console and got out. I felt a little in my own world, in the corridor of connection between the Ponca heavens and the Ponca earth. There was a little stone bench by my uncle's grave, and I went over and sat on it, took a pinch of tobacco in my hand and held it. Aislinn joined me, regarding the scene with her own prodigious gifts.

I ran my eyes over the indescribable grandeur of the land, depositing myself in it, packing away parts of it in my imagination for later, sensing the invisible, deathless history, loving it because love was the key to understanding all such ancient things, and then I began to sing.

The song that came was a prayer song I'd semi-recently learned and I sang it like every bit of it, every word of it, was sacred food and medicine for all the relatives who were there, in all their many forms, from all their different times and eras. Some were healthy and vibrant, some were lost and lonely, some towered, some rested, some were crying, some were beaming love to me, aware of the places in my spirit where I was crying. My song grew louder, streaming out to the furthest tree-covered hills, pouring down our cemetery like a thick shimmering liquid, sprouting into a thousand beautiful black butterflies, all of them riding the winds like young Indian braves riding dragons, all of it made of the purest hope.

Following the spirits, I finished that song and then went right into another one, belting it out, my body getting larger so that I could send a song that was even louder and more faceted than what I normally could. I stood and put some tobacco on my uncle's grave, sprinkling it over the empty beer cans, shells, coins, and other trinkets that had been left as offerings. I took more tobacco from my pouch and kept singing, walking and offering some to this relative's grave and that relative's grave, and then I began to head down past our car to where the majority of our graves were, and all the unnatural-looking small, uprooted trees that Stacy had mentioned.

I'd done this countless times before, but never quite like this. I continued to sing and felt like I was in a trance that would keep going for as long as my singing went unbroken. I went to the obelisk that marked the burial site of all the returned bones and objects from UNL, the ones Grandpa Sammy had been called in to do ceremony for. I went to Aljo's grave, Sonny's, Willie's, relatives whose funerals I'd attended. I went to the headstones of others I didn't know, looked at their faces, read their names, wove through the rows and gnarled trees, putting tobacco on many of them, singing like it was all I had but in my heart I knew that it was enough.

I walked around, sprinkled tobacco, descended the hillside, was a Ponca with a mosaic of other Ponca alive inside me, was a pipe-carrier praying for peace and healing to come to my People, that we could birth a future from the healed best of ourselves and let go of everything we didn't want to be a part of our lives anymore. I was vibrating, sweaty, stretched across numerous points in time, was pitiful, devoted. Aislinn was behind me, praying, offering her own tobacco, in her own zone. I cut to the lowest corner to put some tobacco on my baby cousin Jacob's grave, because I had vowed never to forget him, vowed to always keep his memory alive.

Another song came and I stood looking down at three blank fist-sized bricks that were all in a jagged line together and sort of lost in the grass. I was sad that I couldn't remember which of the three were Jacob's anymore, my memory of his funeral from over thirty years ago too far away to retrieve such things from; I was sad that he'd lived less than a year before he was killed in an alcohol-related homicide, and that no one had ever gotten him a headstone; I wasn't sure anyone but me even visited him anymore. I drizzled the tobacco on the brick that I thought was his and then onto the others too, singing, praying that any who needed to be free from their grief and sadness finally could be. And I kept going, visiting the oldest graves, offering the rest of my tobacco liberally, believing in the power of what we could do for each other, believing in the Creator and the unconditional love that was ultimately waiting for us all. I sang until I was finished and had visited most of the graves, and then I stopped and slowly walked back up to our car in the uncoiling silence, a prayerful man in a beautiful, fading vision.

I sat in the car waiting for Aislinn, crammed in there with our ceremony stuff and camping gear, dripping sweat.

"Where do you want to be buried?" Aislinn has asked me in the past.

"I want to be buried in Niobrara, at the Ponca cemetery," I've replied back. "I want to be buried with my People."

We drove out under the PONKA CEMETERY sign and onto the gravel road, otherworldly colors swirling behind us, translucent hands waving goodbye, our emotions trailing out the open windows, the world ahead silent and haunted in its own way, welcoming us back. I was at the wheel, finally ready to make our go for Columbus and my brother's loud, overly air-conditioned house.

"We're going to have a lot to talk about after this trip, aren't we?" Aislinn asked, lovingly putting her hand out for me to meet and hold.

I thought of all the things I'd experienced at the Sundance, all the different spirits who'd come and what they'd told me; our humble arbor in need of repair, the young dancers who'd made it, the reunion I'd had with my Hunka-brother Mike who'd ran the dance in my twenties. I wanted to tell her all of it but knew, with the new experience content already moving into place, I probably wouldn't get around to it. Like so much I experienced, I'd just store it away, packing it into my soul's bundle.

"Yup," I said, gently squeezing her hand, "we're going to be motor-mouthing about this trip for days and days. We might even have to skip a few nights' sleep just so we can fully get it all out of our system, fully tell every single last good ceremony story we got. No sleep till all the Sundance stories are told!"

Aislinn fake-headbanged, yelling, "No sleep till Brooklyn!" and I cruised past the powwow grounds, smiling and glancing at everything one last time, telling it all that I'd be back, to save me a seat on the bleachers, to get a few good intertribals ready, to make sure the best Indian taco vendor came this year, to hold onto the medicine dreams they had for me until I'd digested my Sundance experience and had made the proper spiritual room for more. I peeled myself away from the receding grounds and prayed silently, asking the ancestors to help me, please, to make it back for the powwow.

"I liked what brother Josh said this year," I said.

"What was that?"

"He said that when hardship comes up, if you can hang in there, there'll always be a reward for you afterwards."

I half-stopped at the stop sign and swung onto the next road.

"All of this," I said, glancing over at her, "feels like a sweet reward to me."

HITTING UP
THE PONCA POWWOW

MY BIG FRAME WEDGED into a tight little airplane seat, enormous cloudscapes hovering around us, I pondered the Ponca powwow. I'd missed the last five, caught the pictures in the newsletter, a little bit of the livestream, but it wasn't the same. I ached. I held fast. I'd been tough and durable since my youth; the guy who could take it. But I missed dropping down into that pool of our People's gathering, sinking deep, my every pore filled with the sights and sounds of Niobrara. I yearned for home.

I put my earbuds in and pressed play on a podcast interview with Chelsea T. Hicks, an Osage writer who'd just come out with a short story collection I wanted to read. Above my head was a piece of luggage packed with ninety copies of *The Memory of Souls*, which the tribe had invited me to give a talk about at the powwow; in fact, they were paying my way out there, and without their check I never would've been able to make it back. Chelsea talked about her goals with her book, and I was carried away, letting her chatty eloquence wash over me. I felt the aims of my little book and imagined Ponca roaring to life with interest in our Ponca culture and ceremonies, language and spirituality. A medicine memoir alive with stories; an old voice finding its way to you from across the campfire, picking the lock on all the things colonization never wanted you to know.

I stared at the seat in front of me and felt grateful to be going back to Nebraska.

We sat in my brother's backyard, circled around an outdoor table, hot and sweaty. My brother was still hulking tough but had put on some drinker's weight. My dad was proud to be with his two sons and two grandchildren, but he still looked rough in his buttoned-up long-sleeved shirt and shorts, smoking his cigarette. My niece Morgan, newly a legit high school teenager, slumped down in her chair, pouring her attention into her phone. I was proud that I wasn't smoking on this trip, blossoming into big-picture communion with the land and skies and memories of my hometown whenever I could, taking my job as rememberer and storyteller seriously.

"Come get me, Uncle Cliff!" Ryder yelled.

It was so cute. While standing at the Arrivals curb in Omaha, lost in my own phone, I suddenly heard, "I missed you, Uncle Cliff," from five-year-old Ryder, who was sticking his head out the open back window of my brother's truck. I love that little rascal/berserker/hellraiser.

Heavier than I was during last summer's visit, I rose from my chair, watched Ryder glance back at me and then keep running away from us in the fenced-in backyard.

"Okay!" I yelled after him. "I had a dream that I was the Flash last night, so you better watch out!"

I started slowly stalking/running toward him as the little guy zipped around the side of the house to where his overgrown and outgrown playset was. I was the peaceful Bigfoot Uncle coming to get my little wild dinosaur-loving nephew.

"Ryder!" I yelled out like a Native Jack Nicholson in *The Shining*. "I'm coming to get you!"

He squealed.

I picked up the pace, sniffed the air, and ran.

My dad and I cruised along Highway 81, his vehicle packed with our powwow gear and a whole bunch of other miscellaneous stuff he just liked to proudly keep in there, like a never-used saw and some spare boots. My dad was coming around, becoming a regular at our Sundance, talking more about Indian stuff than he ever had, and, although grumpy as ever, being about as self-tamed and non-explosive as he'd ever been. I'd wanted a different dad for about two decades, lost him to prison for a decade, and now actually felt like I had a dad and was connecting with him. I stared out the window and listened to him talk non-stop.

"See, you gotta keep your eyes open. That was a big patch of sage right there. We'll have to stop and maybe get some on our way back. I try to tell Misti to collect some sage for her kids but she don't listen. She's just like Vince half the time, worthless."

My poor dad just goes on and on about how worthless everyone is, how mismanaged the tribe is, how so few are as Ponca as he is because he grew up as a kid roughing it all over Niobrara, and how the world is a shitty mess from top to bottom in general. It was his disposition, the prison cut of his character. I remained positive and artful with my conversation, but I'd be lying if I said it didn't wear on me after hours and hours.

"Is Vince going to make it to the powwow?" My dad was the oldest of seven and Vince was the youngest brother, second youngest overall. He had some drug-related brain-troubles, but I loved seeing him.

"Nope," my dad said, almost offended. "He's already said he ain't going. And I'm not going to pick him up."

"One of these days I might have to pop in and check up on him."

My dad stayed silent, a forest of torment and pain and trauma burning eternally in the back of his psyche. Last time I saw Vince, he told me some family stories I'd never heard before. They glowed pricelessly within me.

"Yup," I said, "I'll scoop him up and take him fishing. Split a six-pack of Pepsi with him and get him talking, get him to tell me some stories."

My dad stared ahead.

"Probably only talk if you brought him a six-pack of beer, him."

I cut him off, smiling.

"Well, Budweiser it'll have to be then."

We took the last turn, driving toward the powwow grounds, and I felt giddy, excited. My dad had his armor on, was protecting himself, but I was kind of emotionally leaving him behind, allowing myself to feel as much as there was to be felt, sprouting wings, blasting open with ancestral energies, expanding into a Godzilla-sized set of arms hugging the whole proceedings, and getting hugged back too. The grounds were active, full, cars, RVs, tents, vendors all situating and prepping for the once-a-year gathering. I tried to take in every shining detail.

"I wonder how far Derek and Morg are behind us," my dad asked, slowing, turning into the grounds, prickling up at all that this meant to him.

"I'll send him a text in a little bit," I replied back, glancing at our historic agency building, remembering a little Native boy having a full-on past-life memory recall experience that he shared with Dad and me on those steps at a funeral, remembering the service we'd had for my grandpa there, how I got up and spoke for him at my grandma's request.

"Geeze, there's a lot of people here already," I said. "Can't believe I haven't been to the powwow in five years. It feels like everything's grown."

We drove slowly through the main road that half-circled the grounds, nodding at people, checking things out, acclimating, and internally sniffing out our spot in the groove of it all. People were happy, overheated, tired, taking it easy. They'd tried to erase us but now we were alive and adapted in greater numbers than when they'd first encountered us. I used my Godzilla-arms to give everything another big hug.

"We better go see that Standing Bear statue," my dad said, ready to touch ground in his own way. "Make sure it's being well taken care of."

It was Grand Entry, and I was perched on my piece of the bleachers, surrounded by more Taylors than I'd probably been in a decade. Misti, Miles, Cece, Miles's baby, Shelia, Tiffany, Tiffany's baby, me, Derek, Dad, Morgan, and Ryder. If every Taylor still kicking was there, we would've been way more than a hundred strong. But we were broken apart, scattered, feuding, homeless, and not connected in the same way since my grandpa's passing. The drummers sent their songs flying out to the edges of the world and we all vibrated, our attention on the dancers in their regalia, milling about and looking beautiful.

I turned to Derek, who was a pair of crossed-fingers in a tank top, hoping that Ryder wouldn't go nuts, and said, "I think this is the most dancers I've ever seen at the powwow. Was there this many last year?"

Derek squinted his eyes at the huge mass of colorful people. "Nope. Not that I remember. This is a lot."

A younger guy was at the front, carrying a staff of eagle feathers, followed by two men carrying flags, one of whom was just wearing a shirt with the sleeves cut off and some baggy jeans that were way too big for him. It was beginning. The emcee was directing. People were moving. There was so much I didn't understand.

Probably a lot could've been explained to me, but too many years had gone by without me asking and I was too old to suffer looking dumb now, or something like that. The rest of the dancers began to file in behind my uncle Dennis Lewchuk, and I just appreciated them all, silently thanking every last one of them for learning what they needed to learn so that they could get out there and dance wearing all those feathers and beads and shawls and leggings and moccasins. Was I really too old? Maybe someday that'd be me out there.

We all bounced and rumbled with the drum as the arena filled with the dancers, embodying our tribe's spirit, helping us to feel it, to understand how much we were all a part of it too. It was casual and sacred, a quiet wind and a sky-devouring thunderstorm.

"Uncle Cliff, I want to dance!" Little Ryder said, bright with the energy of it all.

"I'll take you out there," I answered him. "There's these songs called 'intertribals' where everyone can go out there. That's when you and I will dance, okay?"

Little Ryder and I danced semi-in-rhythm with all the other circling relatives, me holding his tiny hand, trying to talk-guide him along through the experience, the cloud-collaged sky spread magnificently overhead.

"Just keep following along, neph," I said. "You're doing great."

We went slow, bounced with the drum like two drops of mercury on the grass speaker of the earth, interweaving with the fully realized superstars stepping and shaking around us. Ryder was such the contrarian that he was struggling to keep himself in line, to not just fire himself against the grain for the sheer principle of it. His spirit wanted to join the ornate turning wheel of proud dancers, but his personality wanted him to knock some things over, roll on the ground, cause a little ruckus and a scene.

He flipped behind me so that his butt was to me and then he tried to dance backwards, keeping his little heels complicatedly close to the backs of mine. I tried to roll with it, stay with the knowing, resplendent flow.

"Uncle Cliff! Don't rub your butt on me, Uncle Cliff!"

I let his small, reversed form continue to shadow and mimic mine. I was having a good time. I've always loved putting myself out into the circle, allowing myself to rise up into the big space of it, to palpably and spiritually be among the thousands who were there with us. I was a cloud in the sky, a star in the Milky Way, an ancestor in Eternity, and I could feel it while I was out there dancing.

"Come on now, Ryder," I said to him, trying to rein him in a bit. "Come back this way. We might fall over and trip some people if we keep dancing like this."

He resisted and then relented, rejoining me at my side. He was probably sensitive like me, overstimulated. Lots of young Natives feel the spirits and energies of the Other World without knowing that they are, and then without the proper understanding and cultural training to handle it and work with it, it just overwhelms them and kind of drives them a little crazy. We crossed between this tough Black afroed dancer and this slow-stepping grandma, and I wondered if Ryder would walk with medicine like I did someday, if he would maybe even take it further than I have.

"You got the moves, Bud!" I told him. "You're fantastic!"

He smiled at me, and I radiated some love back to him. What an honor it was to take him out into the arena for his first dance ever. I hoped he'd remember it, remember this little intertribal with his uncle. I knew that I would.

"Who's the bomb dot com, Ryder? Look at the clouds! Listen to the drum! Isn't this fun?"

I thundered past the most popular frybread stand and the vendor selling all the pelts and skins, heading back to my dad's vehicle to get a book for somebody who wanted to buy one. It was evening time but still brutally, mercilessly hot. I was drinking a ton of water but starting to feel almost a little shaky, which was a bit strange for me as I'm pretty much made of cast iron.

"Are you Cliff?"

I'm always a little jarred when someone I don't know stops me in a public place, indicating that they know me in some way. I looked at the young man with frizzy black-brown hair, beaded choker, and glasses—if he'd been wearing a vest and it was the '70s, he might've just been returning from Woodstock—and couldn't place him.

I nodded my head.

"It's Grandpaboy."

Oh. I recognized his name as the Instagram handle of a young Ponca who followed me.

"From Instagram!"

He nodded. "You said to say hi."

"I did."

He was coming into focus. The half of me that was already digging through my luggage for a book returned to me and helped me to see him more fully. He was soft, clean, educated, queer, and positive-hearted. Like a cool Ponca I'd meet at a coffee shop back in Lincoln on an open-mic night.

"When did you get here?" I asked him.

"Just now. I drove nine hours straight from Denver."

"Whoa. Did you come by yourself? Do you know anybody?"

"I came by myself. And no, I don't know anybody. This is actually the first powwow I've ever been to."

I tried to place his age, saw that he was young. Then I remembered all the times I was a loner somewhere and a relative pulled me in, included me, introduced me to their people as their friend even when we'd just met, and how important that was to my lost self, how therapeutic, essential, and affirming.

"Well, I'm getting a book for someone. Why don't you wait here a second and then come sit with me and my family. There's plenty of room. I'll introduce you to everyone."

He reminded me of myself: eager, youthful, drawn to the culture for all the right, hopeful reasons.

"Like they say in the horror movies," I said to him, as he stood there so full of trust and openness, "I'll be right back."

I made my way to my dad's vehicle, feeling the most at-home at our powwow that I ever have.

If I wasn't surrounded by so many other people, including all my family, I would've teared up and maybe even cried while listening to Robin Bair speak on behalf of a family that was out in the arena and ready to wipe away their tears after a year of mourning. He was built like an Indian Conan, his long gray bundle of hair tied back and electrified behind him, dressed in a tank top, basketball shorts, and what looked like a brand-new pair of expensive, light-brown work boots. A big force moved through him as he talked; some Natives who'd lived their devotion to the culture and ways long enough became passionate instruments of the unseen during such moments, conveying entire worlds. A part of me was in quiet awe, feeling the power of what was traveling into all of us with his every word, spittle flying, chin up, mic in his paw like he was ready to paint-up and go to war for what he was talking about.

"Come out and support your relatives when we go out there. These are hard times, and we need to be there for each other. These are our ways. We are not meant to be alone with our pain and grief. This relative should've never died. This was a tragedy, but we are all here for the family now. Remember the People. Stand up. Come out and dance with us."

He handed the mic back to the emcee, the drummers started up, and slowly the crying family began to dance, with Robin leading the way, his every step shaking the earth, his eyes on things we couldn't see, his whole body dancing forward like a combination of exquisite ancient choreography and total bloody lance-bearing warrior-protector spirit. He moved like the finest Sundance leaders I've ever known, precise, containing the Otherworldly power that was channeling through him, more than human, pure hallucinatory beauty.

A couple at a time, people from under the arena floated out and joined Robin and the family, shaking their hands, hugging them, and then following in step behind them, growing line after line of supportive relatives.

I turned to my new Instagram friend, who was sitting behind Ryder and me on the bleachers, and asked him, "You wanna go out there?"

He thought for a moment and then nodded yes.

"Okay," I said. "Let's go."

The first night of the powwow was behind us and I semi-slept on the bed in the casino hotel room that I'd be sharing with my dad, while Ryder and Morgan watched cartoons from the bed they'd be sharing with Derek. Both my dad and brother were gambling, going out to my brother's truck to drink beers, having their adult fun-bonding time. I think I had heat exhaustion from being out in the hundred-plus-degrees all day. I felt like I was spinning in some underwater hell.

I woke up in the middle of the night and my dad was snoring beside me. I felt awful, got up and turned off the crazy, strobing cartoons on the big screen TV. My stomach churned. I felt like I'd drank too much, and I hadn't had a drink in years and years. I laid down, experienced my stomach revolving in me, felt like retching, couldn't get comfortable, worried that I might have to cancel my talk the next day. "Wouldn't that be fucked," I thought, "if I managed to get all the way across the country on practically no money and then when it came time for my event, to really enjoy the one full day of the powwow, I just got sick and had to hang out in the hotel room all day?"

I prayed, slipped into agony, felt like throwing up whenever I tried to sleep on either of my sides. A half hour or so passed. Then, it felt like it was time for that old drinker's maneuver. Man, it'd been a while since I'd done it . . .

I hauled myself into the bathroom, knelt down, and stuck my fingers down my throat, pushed and kept at it until a little yellow vomit and stomach acid came up; forced myself to do it a couple more times to make sure that I got it all. I then brushed my teeth and immediately felt about 70 percent better.

I got into bed and tried to get comfortable—I didn't like how high the air conditioning was on. I prayed, felt relief, hoped a night's sleep would miraculously fix whatever was happening with me, and then I crashed out.

It was morning time, and I felt strangely, almost completely normal, like I hadn't been grotesquely sick the previous night at all. I couldn't explain it but was grateful. I sipped my coffee and smiled with my whole being in sweet appreciation.

We were visiting my cousin Levi, whom my brother had grown up with as a best friend, going to juvenile detention with him in Kearney for a year and everything, and his wife and kids and dad, who were all camped out together in Niobrara State Park, which was maybe two miles from the powwow grounds. Levi was a stud, an inspirational speaker of sorts, always doing athletic challenges and feats online to pump people up about believing that they really could change their lives. I dug him. When Aislinn and I were back the month before, the three of us had a deep talk, full of all the things the spirits really want for us to have on our minds and in our consciousness. He ate it up and I invited him and his family to come to our Sundance the next year.

My dad pulled up, having gone off to pick up another gigantic Indian relative he'd known all his life, Levi's dad's brother. Some more folks showed up. Levi said to his game and slender wife, "See, now it's switched, and you get to feel how I feel when I'm doing everything with your big family, as the only non-white guy. Here, you're the only white person among a bunch of rugged Indians, haha." He laughed and she took a drink of her beer. Everybody was laughing. Everybody was drinking too except for me and the kids. A kind of love and long history and childhood connections and grown boys proud to be with their fathers and secret powwow soul sauce seemed to pervade the busy campsite. We were imperfect, some of us haunted, but we were together, and that togetherness seemed to both sum up and radiantly express everything our Ponca hearts believed.

Levi smiled at me, saying, "Cliff, you gotta tell us another Bigfoot story. Those ones you told at the cabin were for real."

I could feel the Bigfoot that were walking with Levi and his family, that wanted me to pass along certain stories and kinds of knowledge. They were robust and earthy, far-seeing, fierce, particular about who they extended their guardianship to, their hairy forms glowing with depthless love like a vast night sky glowing with the light of a swollen full moon. These were the beings who were among us as we joked and drank and kept the morning-time conversation rolling.

"Well, lemme think of one," I said, reclining back in my cheap camping chair. "I know I've gotta help you build up your family's collection. I know that's what these Bigfoot would want."

I sipped my coffee, thought, and they drank, and laughed.

I sat beside Melvin Frasier Sr. back behind all the loud powwow joy, by the little groundskeeper home he'd lived in for the last twenty years, the home my late uncle Sandy had lived in before him. My dad didn't care for Melvin and his family in the slightest, to put it lightly, but I didn't mind. I was interested in connecting with whomever I was interested in connecting with, following my own instincts, honoring my own twenty-some-year active journey of cultural and ceremonial explorations; all my dad's crap could ride in his backseat, but it wasn't welcome in mine. My dad did tell me that my grandpa Cliff babysat Melvin Sr. when he was a little kid; I did always think that was cool. Melvin smoldered with quiet. I bobbed in it too, waiting for the right thoughts to come.

"We gonna have a sweat tonight, after the powwow?" I asked. We'd always had a sweat up in the buffalo pasture about midnight on Saturday after everyone had either gone to sleep or relocated elsewhere to go drinking. I looked forward to it all year; praying in the heart of the homelands with a clutch of other Ponca. Melvin always led the ceremony.

"No, I don't think so," he said. "Not this year."

He was a shade of dark brown somewhere between my dad's and mine. He wore a red headband and a beaded medicine pouch that hung at the center of his chest. He'd cared for our tribe's buffalo herd for the last twenty years. He was gentle, old, had thick hands, seemed ready to step back and let others take over.

"The fire folks came out and said no open fires. It's too dry out. Not even a sweat fire."

"I guess there's always next year."

It's a skill to fit your silence into the uncontrived silence of an Elder you're sitting with, a skill that everyone should have, like knowing how to love animals and control your anger. It's the way to meet what that one-of-a-kind Elder has in them to share, the way to meet their shining soul. Such things should be a regular part of all people's lives. I folded my silence into his.

"Where are you staying?" he asked me, looking forward at the powwow personnel rattling by on their expensive little golf-cart-on-steroids.

"I stayed last night in the casino with my dad and brother and the kids, but I was thinking of staying here tonight."

"You got a tent?"

"Yeah, but I haven't set it up yet."

"You ever sleep in a tipi?"

I hadn't. There was a long story about the time I tried to and almost did, but I hadn't.

"Well, if you want you can sleep in that one behind us. No one's sleeping in it yet. We just put it up."

"Really?"

"Yeah."

I settled into the mood of all that was present.

"Dang, then I guess I might."

I stood with my hands politely folded in front of me, listening to my great aunt Debbie as she talked to me. She sat on the seat of her walker, her big form resting and somewhat worrisome. She was my grandpa Cliff's youngest sister, his last sibling remaining. We were under the arbor at the spot reserved for the Elders. The powwow was breathing, unfurling, paused.

"I have this picture for you. I heard that you were coming and knew that I would see you."

She reached into the side pocket of her walker and handed me a glossy portrait with two olden-time Indians on it, a man and his wife. A little grandkid ran up and hugged her. Throughout our whole exchange a vibrant assortment of grandkids did this, peppering her with love, receiving hugs from her.

"Now that's your grandpa's grandpa," she said. "Do you know him?"

I didn't. I felt like I was shivering under a buffalo robe, standing in the snow, listening to my ancestors.

"Uh uh," I replied. "I only know his dad, Alex Taylor, and nothing further back than that."

"Well, this is where you got that Taylor name from. This man here"—I held out the picture and she tapped on it with her finger—"is Moses Taylor. And you know what else? He was an enrolled Chippewa."

All this time and, as far as I knew, no one in my family had ever mentioned that we had Chippewa blood. I saw the flush blue sky open up and a new face peered down at me, 1800s-looking and loving.

"So, I'm part Chippewa?"

"Yes, you are. Not even your dad knew that until I told him just a little bit ago. You keep this. See, I got all sorts of things to tell you, but you don't come over to visit me. You gotta come visit so I can tell these stories before I'm gone. Call me on the phone sometime."

Another itty-bitty grandkid came over and got some love. I felt some pain for all the conversations and invitations I didn't follow up on, and how so many of those relatives were now passed; I felt a tightness in my heart over how much was expected of me, how people had always known I was smart and spiritual and wanted me to become a repository for everything that was in danger of vanishing.

"Your uncle Sandy had his enrollment number in his papers, but when the new culture director came in it got lost. But now you have this much. You gotta find that number and do some more research. Figure out who you are."

The one-legged emcee got to speaking loudly on his mic and I held my response as another woman older than me came up to embrace my aunt Debbie. I felt a grief that was stadium-sized, ocean-of-dead-buffalo sized, tribe-wide and spanning the generations. How to learn all the stories? How to gather and collect them all?

The emcee made an announcement that I'd be giving a talk about my book shortly, at 2 p.m. under the shelter (my reading was originally going to be in the agency building but due to Covid it was moved outdoors at the last minute), but it didn't seem to register with too many people as I scanned the stands. It was okay by me. I figured whoever was meant to come and hear me passionately share about what all lived in the story of my book would just be there. My dad sat in his expensive outdoor chair beside me, simmering yet supportive. It wasn't hard for me to feel how proud he was of me, even if he wasn't the best at expressing it.

I told him I'd meet him over there and began to wander off by myself, to peel away from the bristling, spinning, humble, and magnificent activity of the powwow, so that I could shift gears and show up to my gig as the professional I strove to be. I grabbed some books from my dad's vehicle, my tobacco, and silently—with the intention of going into myself and temporarily turning off all the non-stop, profusive socializing—walked over to the tipi Melvin Sr. had invited me to sleep in that night, ducking inside and sighing in the refreshing silence.

Spirits came when I gave my talks, but I never mentioned them, just folded what they showed me into the spontaneous flow of what I was sharing. It was sacred work even if I never explicitly talked about it as such. And over the years I'd learned that it was beneficial to reset myself before a talk, especially if I was coming in from a high-energy super social scene, like the powwow. That was why I had come to the tipi.

I offered some tobacco and prayed, spoke to the Creator, relaxed, surrendered, tossed my words up into the all-loving heavens, felt like an animal about to lick the source of all life, quiet and still and fundamentally happy. I looked at the bits of brown tobacco on the grassy ground and stared like they might suddenly animate and zip out of the tipi's opening.

I didn't have a whole lot of time, so I set the timer on my phone for about ten minutes. A seasoned meditator—maybe someday all Ponca will meditate—could go pretty far in ten minutes, bring their organism into a restful stillness of pure peace and Spirit perception. Care for yourself, use your gifts, and then see what happens.

I closed my eyes, breathed in the uniqueness and cultural beauty of the tipi, and then quickly became a lake of pure consciousness without any ripples.

I sat on top of a silver steel picnic table that hadn't been wiped off after lunch and gave my talk, peering into space, rumbling with the not-too-distant powwow drums, and occasionally meeting eyes with the small number of folks who were there, including my dad, the tribe's photographer and her boyfriend, and then a few other friends and relatives. I'd hoped for some more folks to show but after waiting twenty minutes and beginning with just three listeners, I just went for it, opening up my gift and going where the spirits guided me.

It was kind of like being in a lucid, layered, very stable vision. I was cranking out my story, speaking the truths and understandings I'd been given in the very location where parts of my memoir had taken place, in this old Ponca land where so many of our ancestors dwelled and continued to develop, in this beautiful river country where the family lines of all us Ponca met and rooted into the earth, knotting together into one ancient old source bundle. I told my story so that its medicine could rain down on all of us, because it was a thing larger than me, entrusted to me, meant in its design to reach all corners and dimensions of our People, even if it heavily featured me and my family and friends and people I'd known. I felt my words traveling far, winging up hills, spiriting through time, going into ears, slipping into hearts, expanding people's consciousness, becoming clothes, bulking up culture, vanishing into the light of our buffaloes' eyes, riding the wind, pasting on the babies like chewed-up plant medicines, drenching parts of many Ponca across space and time that hadn't been touched by such things in a long, long time.

I gave myself over to what was happening. I teared up while telling the pair of dreams in which the spirits actually wrote the book I was holding, describing how they put it into my body afterwards and told me that I had to then write it for the people in this material world. I glanced up at my dad and saw all that he was feeling while his son spoke of these sacred things at our powwow where we were all fighting to overcome what had happened to us and what had been stolen from us, by beautifully being ourselves and coming together again and again as Ponca People. I saw my deceased uncle Ronnie Picotte right over in the spot where we'd had our last talk, that summer after my dad went to prison; Ronnie was smiling, cheering me on with the kind of love that our relatives are capable of fully realizing and embodying on the Other Side, making me want to cry some more but I held back. I felt into the pieces of the CENTER that everyone there at the powwow had brought with them, that were circling and cohering into a multidimensional pulsing heart of grief and joy and hope, and I made my every word a precious, selfless, storytelling thing modeled after that holy center's sweet, aching essence.

I held my little book about the little people and the Sundance in my hand and I told the stories that all the many ancestors around me wanted me to tell.

Deep and kind of lost in my storyteller's medicine trance, and wildly in love with my People, our realness, our sacredness, our beautiful way of being, I suddenly caught my favorite little dude running across the cement floor of the shelter right on over to me, interrupting me, breaking me out of what was happening for a few seconds, like some child trickster wearing a coyote's head wanting to make sure that I put a little of what he had to say into my big world-making story too.

"Are you done yet?" Ryder asked, genuinely bothered.

I looked down at him with affection. I loved this nephew so much. I couldn't wait until there was a Cliff the Fourth, my own little boy making my life difficult and infinitely better.

"When are you going to stop talking, Uncle Cliff?"

He was almost exasperated; maybe he didn't like all the attention being on me. I knew that that was what his dad and sister would say.

"I'm almost done," I kind of lied, placating him. "Just wait over by your dad and I'm going to wrap this up."

His voice trailed over his shoulder as he ran back to his dad, who was shaking his head. "Okay, Uncle Cliff!"

"Hey! I heard you got a book out. I want a copy."

It was my uncle Vance Appling, short and stocky, dressed in full buckskin, adorned with about five painted turtle shells, including a shield and a codpiece. More than a couple readers mentioned how much they loved his cameo in my book, as the lightning-struck story-sharing heavy-metal-loving buffalo hide tanner. Like so many who were at the powwow that I'd been seeing since I was a kid, I was just glad that he was still alive.

"Holy shit!" I said, overjoyed. "What's up, Vance!"

We were by the Crow's Nest, where they were selling powwow t-shirts. I had a bag full of books and Hobby Lobby book-selling stuff I'd made, and I had a small folded-up card table—so much was going on but that's the way it was: you were journeying out into the psychedelic sea of it all and then you were stopping and vanishing into these clear moments and conversations.

"I didn't think I was going to get here. I just had my third surgery on my foot. I got gangrene bad. The doctor said I wouldn't be walking till, at best, next week, but to hell with that. I knew I had to be here for Grand Entry. And I've been out there dancing almost every round. Foot hurts like a beast though. But I'm used to that. What about a book? I follow what you're doing online. The Indian Club y'all started is way cool. You're doing all the right things. I'm a storyteller too, but I just don't have the talent for putting it all down into words. I love to tell the story of how the Sundance came to us, piss some people off with my version too, haha, but that can't be helped."

We chatted away and were visited by memories of the summer when we really hung out, when he told me a number of stories that made it into my book. I felt like we were both blooming where we stood; crazy were-wolf Ponca men bursting into beautiful bouquets of flaming Nebraska wildflowers. I would never quit living in complete admiration of all our Indian People who were such supernaturally gifted storytellers, humbly and gloriously functioning as local living tribal libraries, preserving the soul of everything, like my lightning-struck uncle Vance. Suddenly, I did something I never do . . .

I set my card table down, pulled my phone from my pocket, and asked him, "Can I get a picture of us together?"

Vance was all whiskers, smiles, turtle shells, bent guy, and spirit power.

"Of course, brother! Let me fix myself up."

He got to adjusting himself, fixing his hair, his many necklaces, his shells.

I set the rest of my stuff down, turned to my dad, who'd been quietly standing there all along. "Dad, can you take our picture?"

"All right," he said. "I'm not very good but I'll try."

People kept talking to me and my dad where I'd talked with Vance for quite a while, so I wound up just setting my table and stuff down right there, in the orbit of the Crow's Nest, not in the main path of everyone but still visible and set apart. I didn't totally know what I was doing but I followed the confidence I was feeling, my bright sense of purpose. I taped a red sign that said PONCA WRITER on the part of my table that would catch the most eyes, displayed my book on a stand, placed two stacks of books toward the front, and then used a stone to hold down a big sheet of construction paper on which I'd written my book's description in black marker. It was bare bones, but I felt like it could do everything I needed it to do for the next couple hours (whatever that was, haha).

Immediately, people began to come over, seeing me, seeing my book, picking it up, looking it over, asking me questions. "You're Ponca? You wrote this? Are you the writer the tribe did the post about online? How long did it take you to write this? What do you mean little people? How much is it? Can I Venmo you?"

I turned on all my long-time cashier's customer-service charisma and met everyone who came up with joy, sincerity, humor, genuine interest, and a touch of contrarian moxie just to honor everything that couldn't fit into each conversation or interaction. The energy of the powwow guided folks over to me, young rez kids, old white women, grungy hermits who'd emerged from the hills just for the day, slow-talking Indians, a Sundance brother from Hidden Valley, aunties, my aunt Debbie, my inspiring friend

Barbara who was about to publish her own dream-born series of Niobrara-set books, overly talkative Ponca from California, my Instagram buddy, my cousin Randy and his family whom I hadn't seen since my grandpa's funeral, and on and on. It was crazy, a blast; I felt so tightly woven into the living pattern of my People, so happy to be renewing my connections, and to be making new ones. During those rare moments between customers and conversations, I would just kick back and watch the powwow, try to disappear into it, to nuzzle against its mysterious, busy interior.

I wrote the book for my tribe, to help us along with the great doctoring that was needed, that was happening, so we could all feel proud and strong again, so we could all be spiritually connected again and heal and live in healthy, empowered closeness with our ancestors; and now I was sharing it with everyone at our most essential event, at our biggest gathering. I felt like the little people must've seen this moment when they originally gave me the book in that dream those seven years earlier. I felt like all the parts of my life were in perfect alignment at the most ideal place; I felt like my purpose as a Ponca was being completely fulfilled.

"You know, my family has an actual handwritten letter from Chief Standing Bear's daughter," an elderly white woman told me, holding a copy of my book in her hand. "And I would love for you to read it."

I leaned back in my chair, nodded at my cousin who was walking by, and said, "Wow. I would really love to read that too."

After about four hours and selling about forty books, completely drained from all the constant enthusiastic connecting, I decided to fold up shop. I felt like I was a character in some magical story where my tribe was on the verge of getting everything that we'd lost and more back, where my tribe was about to launch into some beautiful, superpowered, ceremony-and-language, corn-and-chanuppa thick, golden guided LANDBACK future; and heck, maybe I was, maybe we actually were. I put my stuff back in its bag, untaped my sign, and danced a little with the dancers in the arena on the spot of grass that'd been so good to me.

"Are you Cliff?"

I looked up and saw a young, twenty-year-old woman, crowned and dressed in green and blue regalia, wearing glasses like some cynical kid detective, a little acne, proud and tough. I knew who she was but hadn't talked to her in maybe over a decade.

"My mom told me that you dedicated a book to my grandpa."

I nodded. It was Nicole Bad Moccasin's daughter, Joe Bad's granddaughter. Earlier, Nicole had been one of the many people who visited my table; we reminisced about her dad, telling stories from when he was alive and then stories about how he'd been coming to people since he passed; I told her about how he'd come to my last two Sundances, how he came to my sweats back in Oregon.

"Yup, your grandpa had a tremendous impact on my life," I told her. "That's why I dedicated my book to him. He helped an uncountable number of people in his lifetime and is still helping people to this day from the Other Side."

She looked at me like she knew what I was saying was true, but also like she wouldn't be ready to really feel everything that her soul was gathering for her for at least another ten years.

"How much is it?"

"Fifteen bucks."

She looked at the powwow, winding down and thinning out, keeper of traditions, giver of sacred gifts, and then a little piece of something inside her softened.

"Okay," she said. "I'd like one. Can you sign it for me?"

I sat in my dad's vehicle by the Feather Hill gas pumps, eating a cold sandwich, some salty chips, and drinking a Pepsi. We'd made it back to the casino, taking off from the powwow when it officially ended, opting not to go to a little late-night concert featuring my dad's cousin Terry Taylor and his son just because we were both bushed, just too damn tired. I ate like I was starving, trying to give myself some shape back by stuffing it down, devouring my final meal of the day.

Whatever had gotten me the night before remained a mystery. I felt better and normal for most of the day, up for the never-ending marathon of it, my power levels what I needed them to be. I thought about something the spirits told me as I was sitting at my card table, between visitors. They said, *Your medicine attracts the people you're meant to cross paths with, whether it's just for a single interaction or for something that'll last for years. It's like a magnet. Don't worry. It'll bring the people you're fated to meet to you.* And then the very next thing this strapping white farmer comes over and it turns out he's been dating my cousin for years and he's rezoned a hundred and twenty acres of his family farm to be land left alone, land eventually meant to be given back to the Ponca.

"Natives from down South came to visit the land," he told me, "and they saw medicines they hadn't seen in years, growing there just because we've decided to let the land itself decide what she wants to sprout and grow there. It's amazing, humbling." As he talked, my spirit-eyes saw all sorts of things that could maybe happen on that land someday, and I felt the truth of what the spirits had told me just a handful of minutes earlier.

"We better go see what little Venom and Morgie are up to," my dad said, hopping back into the vehicle; still like a piece of rebar, something that would or maybe already had survived the apocalypse.

"Look at that moon," I said, seeing its blood-red orb rising up through the clouds; its nightly appearance a message to the part of us that knew we were supposed to stay strong and follow our soul's light.

"That's pretty cool," he said, putting his overpacked vehicle in gear. "That's exactly how it looked when I was a kid. That's a Niobrara moon."

The next morning, we emptied our crew out of our casino hotel room and went to a café on the edge of Niobrara for breakfast. Derek was ready to head back to Columbus; my dad and I had plans to hang out at the powwow for a little bit longer and then hit up the Ponca-owned Niobrara Market so that he could spend his two-hundred-dollar grocery gift card getting some things (we all got one and you could only spend it there; I gave mine to a Sundance sister who worked at the casino, for her and her cousins to stock up with). We were all feeling a little tired, bittersweet because our powwow for the year was coming to an end.

Our rough-looking gang entered the café, and it was mostly white folks but there were two other tables of Natives, so we decided to go for it. A dynamic and dramatic hostess, who seemed destined for New York City or at least better things, directed us to an open table by one of the other Native tables and we all got settled in. It only took a second for me to see that I knew one of the Natives at the quiet, neighboring table, and I quickly found myself bursting with a little powwow reunion happiness.

"Delrayne!"

She got up and we hugged each other in our cramped corner. She was in her late sixties and still a picturesque, brown-skinned Native beauty. Smooth features, kind smile, long braided black hair; in a powwow t-shirt and jeans.

"It's good to see you, Cliff."

I introduced her to my family, and she introduced us to everyone at her table and then we sat back down and began having our own little conversation, our chairs turned away some from our respective tables. I'd known Delrayne since my early twenties and for the majority of the ten years when my dad was in prison, when just my buddy Dan and I would come up to the powwow, we camped right next to her, discovered a comfort zone for ourselves around the cooking fire with her and the cook and his wife. It was the cook I wanted to ask her about.

"Is Logan Bear here this year?" I asked. "I swear I glanced up and saw him, kind of skinnier and with a cane. I didn't get a chance to talk to him but it kind of looked like him."

"No," she said, a sparkle of memory in her eyes, "it wasn't him. He passed away a couple years ago. He was a dear old soul."

For years I sat by that cooking fire, listening to him talk up a hilarious storm about all manner of things that comprised his life. He was a

Vietnam vet who drove over from Denver. He had a sweet wife named Ida who'd passed a few years before him.

"Man, he would get us laughing with those jokes of his," I said, accepting things, promising myself that I'd remember him far into my old age.

"He was funny, wasn't he?" Delrayne said.

We were both silent for a moment, the café loud around us. I felt so glad to have this little run-in with Delrayne; my powwow experience wouldn't have been complete without it.

"So, when are y'all heading out?" I asked, taking a sip of my coffee. "You sticking around a little longer?"

I sat on the bleachers watching all the dancers shake, step, transform into ancestors, emanate culture, express their soul's power, and waited for one more intertribal so that I could get out there one last time. I was patient, tumbling down into the esoteric depths of our tribe's being even as my ass sat all sore on my steel seat. Enough patience and I could live happily alongside my ancestors before shedding my body. Enough patience and the vision of how all the pieces fit together would come to me. My dad half-lurked behind me. "You about ready to go?" he asked. "We gotta get over to that Market before they close, before they run out of things. I think I'm ready."

It took me a while, but I'd realized that my dad was triggered by being around our People, our tribe, this land he grew up on. He was extra critical, full of complaints, tearing people down, angrily talking shit. He was sincerely getting something from the powwow, no doubt, but a lifetime of pain and grief and anger was also swimming to the surface, like ghosts coming to see if we Ponca were really still around, coming to cry, wail, scream, kill, be heard. Many ancestors came to our powwow, but many ghosts did too.

"I want to try to get in one more intertribal," I told him, half kid, half grown man. Over the past twenty years he'd mellowed with me, set lines he wouldn't cross with me because of love, because he wanted to be in my life; maybe because he was sorry. We got along all right.

"I can't believe Vince didn't make it up here," my dad said, "not even to get that two-hundred-dollar gift card. Out of everybody, he's the one who needs it, too."

I watched the dancers circle, felt the drumbeat hammering me, looked closely at the faces of the younger ones, sunk into my prayers, wished for things, grieved inside, heard the whispers of the spirits, was grateful to be there with my dad. Patience could create healing just like plants and the Medicine People did. Patience could create healing just like the hands of the Creator themselves did.

I wanted to wait for that next intertribal, but I was also used to sacrificing my own wants and needs for others (and not always in a healthy way), so I relented and told him, "Yeah, let's get going."

"You sure?" he said, the father in him feeling what his son really wanted.

I stood up, surrendering, saying goodbye.

"Yup," I said, "let's roll."

I was up at 6:30 in the morning. We were back in Columbus. Life had resumed. I drank my Keurig coffee in my brother's darkened living room, his car-hood-sized flatscreen off, waiting for my niece. It was her first day of band practice as a sophomore in high school. My brother was at work, Grandpa and Ryder were asleep. I had volunteered to drive her the next two mornings.

I treasured the family I was in the middle of, was so happy that my brother was providing a better life for his kids than we'd had, while secretly hoping that he'd cut back on his drinking someday. My brother and I were changing the storyline; in our hearts we both knew that that was our purpose.

Morgan emerged from the bathroom all done-up and sharp-looking, like a shy girl ready to impress. I gave her a cool West Coast Indian Uncle smile. “Uncle Greased Lightning says he can get you to the new high school in under sixty seconds. ‘Impossible,’ you say? Not even. Let’s blow this Runza food truck. Aho!”

She looked at me like I was a guy trying to fake read a book that I was unwittingly holding upside down. This was how she looked at me pretty much ever since she entered high school.

I slipped my flip-flops on, and we went out into the blinding morning sunshine, crunched our faces at it, got in Derek’s car and hit the road. “You wanna get some Burger King quick?” I asked her. Her expression loosened.

“Naw, we don’t got time for anything like that, haha.” She was over me. Not everything I said landed. There I was again, forever trying to redeem myself.

We drove past a small trailer court, some low-energy road construction, a few gorgeous houses, cruising along in a current of real love and old memories and teenage worlds I both knew and had no clue about. Morgan looked at her phone while I made the conversation, drank my coffee, and scrutinized the growth and happenings of my old hometown. For whatever reason, neither of us said much about the powwow, despite it being there in the backseat as a trio of interested, head-bobbing Ponca ancestors.

“You gonna need me to pick you up?” I asked, making the turn to the new high school. “Maybe we can sneak over to Burger King then?”

She kept her gaze fixed into her phone. “No, I’ll get a ride back with my friend.”

“Cool,” I said, staring at the blue sky for a long second, drifting someplace I had no words for; a homeworld, something beyond that even.

“Make good decisions and follow your creativity and you’ll be set, all right?”

I was always saying stuff like this to her, hoping that some of it stuck, and that it would maybe help her in the long run as she became her own person and left the origin-story of her Columbus youth behind, just like I did.

We pulled to a stop behind a line of other cars with other kids hopping out.

"Thanks, Uncle Cliff! Bye!"

She shut the door before I could say anything back and then I pulled out of there, smiling and full of all sorts of sweet uncle feelings.

Aislinn slept, as beautiful as the mermaid goddess that she was, and I drove. It was past midnight. I was exhausted. I had started the day off in Nebraska and now I was pushing myself to drive the last fifty miles home. The night squeezed everything. The trees walked the hills just like this one Medicine Man told me they did every night, and I laughed thinking of everything else they must've been doing when us foolish, misguided humans weren't looking.

I actually loved this drive, the valleys, the vibe-shifts, following the shimmering, starlit Columbia River, the twists, familiar landmarks, the sheer number of times I'd driven it something like a poem about going home weaving around me. I'd missed so many Ponca powwows in a row but not anymore; now my inner landscape was fresh with the experience of that holy gathering: vibrant, dripping, humming, hugged, kissed. And next year I'd be back. I looked over at Aislinn—we'd just celebrated our five-year anniversary with a romantic two days in Hood River before I'd left—and loved on her through all my tiredness.

"We want to meet your partner," so many of my relatives at the powwow said.

"She's still never been to a single real powwow in her entire life," I told them. "But next year you'll meet her because we're both coming back."

I rolled the window down and stretched my eyes wide open, let the onrushing air slap me awake. I longed to rest and I longed to do more. I longed for more time with my family and tribe back in Nebraska and I longed to travel, explore, gulp down more from other places too. I longed forward and backward in time simultaneously, stretched between my ancestors and the time when I would be an ancestor someday. I longed in concert with the deep longing inside our Mother Earth, sensing the stories she was reaching for, my place in them, our tribe's place in them, everyone's place in them. I longed and blinked my eyes and drank my fourth coffee and drove as well as I could.

When we got to Astoria, I woke Aislinn up, put my hand on her leg and gently let her know that we'd made it. There were no other cars on the road; a crisp night-time quiet flowed over everything.

"My powwow journey is over, my love," I told her. "We're here."

ACKNOWLEDGMENTS

Previously published on www.lastrealindians.com:

"What Being Ponca Means to Me"

"If We Can't Powwow, Then Let's Go Camping!!!"

"When Thunder Met Lightning: The Story of How I Met My Brother Denny"

Previously published in *Ponca Tribe of Nebraska Member News*:

"What Being Ponca Means to Me"

"If We Can't Powwow, Then Let's Go Camping!!!"

"When Thunder Met Lightning: The Story of How I Met My Brother Denny"

"Some Notes on the Little People"

"The Rain That Wasn't Wet"

Without the help and love of many, neither I nor this book would be here today. I overflow with gratitude when I think of all the people and relatives who've been there for me and contributed to the fulfillment and realization of the dream that this book truly is. To name a few . . .

To the mythological hometown artists crew of the Village Inn corner booth (smoking section) in the late 90s: you helped me find myself at an early age and showed me so much, including how to survive; that art constitutes a viable, sacred way of life; and that true friendships save lives. The dreams of those times continue and, as far as I'm concerned, they always will.

To Clark: you've been there since the beginning (I'll never get over how you were almost named Cliff, right up until that last minute), and I couldn't have asked for a more beautiful brother and friend in this life. You've always been my favorite writer, and no thanks will ever be enough for your invitation to join you in Seattle, a move that allowed for the whole rest of my life to really begin. *What do you say, is there ever gonna be a day, when the captives are set free, and heaven meets us halfway . . .*

To my Taylor family, my grandpa Cliff and grandma Barb, Mark, Alton, Misti, Sheila, and Charmaine: the river of your generations flows into my generation, this book, and beyond. My being radiates with the pain and beauty of our family, and I believe at the heart of all that is a deep living prayer that gave birth to this book. May that living prayer of our family help all who wade into these pages.

To my Hidden Valley Sundance family: you took me in over twenty years ago and helped me to become the Ponca man I was meant to be. Tears of gratitude and joy to brother Mike in the Next World, Simon, Kermit, Beau, Young Simon, brother Josh, who originally invited me and now always gets me back to the airport, and all who come and pray and dance and sing and help out and support year after year. The indestructible ways of our People continue, and it is all ineffable, holy, essential, and astonishing.

To my grandpa Zachariah Boughn: your love has never left me. Gone twenty years, your inspiration is always in the room with me. I told you I wanted to be a writer, and you've helped me to become one. This is our book, Grandpa! We wrote this!

To my brother Denny: Indians and brothers forever, following in the footsteps of Grandpa Sammy, continuing his work, pulling off the impossible, laughing and telling stories and not getting too freaked out by the spirits. Love you. Here's my book; now it's your turn.

To the Handyshop: if a gas station can have a spirit, and I believe they can, then thank you for the ways in which you cared for me, supported my healing, and transformed me into a Poet. Our decade together sings in me whenever I think about it. Thank you and thanks to everyone who was a part of that overnight universe back in the day.

To my brother Derek, niece Morgan, and nephew Ryder: I love you and always will. Seeing you all when I can is a treasure for my heart. We come from hard times but have made it to better times (some of which are depicted in this book). Can't wait to hug y'all and hang out in that hot Nebraska sun again soon.

To my great-great-great grandpa Chief Standing Bear: your life continues to reverberate through all of our Ponca lives. The Great Spirit gave us a great, unforgettable inspiration in you. A role model. A hero. A true Ancestor. A living spiritual grandpa Chief for all of us. Thank you for all the ways you live in my heart and in the hearts of our people. Weblaho!

To the little people: I love walking with you, knowing you, creating with you, and witnessing your work on this beauty-filled earth, who is our Mother. May a healing remembrance of you and your Nations pervade the land, and may many laugh and pray and collaborate and enjoy sacred friendship with you again.

To my Ancestors: before I came into this world we talked, and I have spent my whole life aspiring to make good on what we talked about. Thank you for the miracles you make happen, as well as your everyday comforts, companionship, guidance, protection, and infusions of brilliance. All of us today walk with you knowing that our culture and spirituality is meant to have a future, and a beautiful one. Thank you for giving us so much, including this sacred vision of Hope.

To the Elders, mentors, and Medicine people who've blessed me with all of their love and knowledge: what you gave me is a priceless gift. Char Knoflicek-Bordeaux, Joe Bad Moccasin, Myron Longsoldier: our times together have been character-shaping, and I will remember them always.

To my mom: you raised a good son, you passed on the family love of books, and I love you so much. Thanks, Mom!

To my dad: it's not easy being Indian and you never let us forget that! Without you, neither I nor this book would be walking around in this holy world. Thanks, Dad. Thanks for coming to Sundance with me every year and thanks for your love.

To Aislinn, my beloved: the best eight years of my life have been the last eight years with you. Your heart, your magic, your dedication, and your soul's beauty, all make me fall in love with you a sweet little bit more every day. Thanks for all the ways you help my deepest dreams to become lived realities, including this book and all the others. Thanks for saying yes when I asked you to marry me (twice in Ponca, then once in English). Thank you for being my true love.

To our Ponca People: this book is for us. They tried to kill us, to wipe us from the face of the earth, but our ancestors, the Earth Herself, and the Creator were never going to let that happen. We're here to live lives of beauty, healing, joy, ceremony, and love. We're here to help each other remember and figure out how to do that. My prayer is that this book helps whoever reads it with that most humble and human work.

To the Creator: thank you for this life, for giving me a vision, for your healing, for everything and a million things more, and for helping me to write this book and all the books you've empowered my heart to dream up.

To my editor Suzzanne Kelley and NDSU Press: thank you for sending me the best email of my life, telling me that you wanted to publish my book. Your presence and expertise in the process has been crucial and amazing. Thank you for shepherding this Ponca essay collection into its fully realized book form.

And, last, to everyone who appears in these pages: thank you! Bigfoot Hugs forever and always!!!

ABOUT THE AUTHOR

photo courtesy of Josué Rivas

Cliff Taylor (enrolled member of the Ponca Tribe of Nebraska) is an award-winning writer, poet, speaker, and storyteller. He is the author of a memoir, *The Memory of Souls* (2020), and two poetry collections, *The Native Who Never Left* (2023) and *Notes of an Indigenous Futurist* (2024). A Nebraskan through and through, he currently lives on the Oregon Coast with his sweetheart of many years.

ABOUT THE PRESS

North Dakota State University Press (NDSU Press) exists to stimulate and coordinate interdisciplinary regional scholarship. These regions include the Red River Valley, the state of North Dakota, the plains of North America (comprising both the Great Plains of the United States and the prairies of Canada), and comparable regions of other continents. We publish peer reviewed regional scholarship shaped by national and international events and comparative studies. Neither topic nor discipline limits the scope of NDSU Press publications. We consider manuscripts in any field of learning. We define our scope, however, by a regional focus in accord with the press's mission. Generally, works published by NDSU Press address regional life directly as the subject of study. Such works contribute to scholarly knowledge of region (that is, discovery of new knowledge) or to public consciousness of region (that is, dissemination of information or interpretation of regional experience). Where regions abroad are treated, either for comparison or because of ties to those North American regions of primary concern to the press, the linkages are made plain. Since 1950, NDSU Press has published substantial trade books, but the line of publications is not limited to that genre. We also publish textbooks (at any level), reference books, anthologies, reprints, papers, proceedings, and monographs. The press also considers works of poetry or fiction, provided they are established regional classics or they promise to assume landmark or reference status for the region. We select biographical or autobiographical works carefully for their prospective contribution to regional knowledge and culture. All publications, in whatever genre, are of such quality and substance as to embellish the imprint of NDSU Press. We changed our imprint to North Dakota State University Press in January 2016. Prior to that, and since 1950, we published as the North Dakota Institute for Regional Studies Press. We continue to operate under the umbrella of the North Dakota Institute for Regional Studies, located at North Dakota State University.

THE CONTEMPORARY VOICES OF INDIGENOUS PEOPLES SERIES

North Dakota State University Press initiated the Contemporary Voices of Indigenous Peoples Series (CVIP) in 2016. The series was first co-edited by Drs. Suzzanne Kelley and Michael Yellow Bird, a citizen of the Three Affiliated Tribes of the Fort Berthold reservation in North Dakota. He identifies as Arikara (The People) and Hidatsa (Willows). Michael retired from our series—having served from 2016 to 2023—and relocated to Winnipeg. His successor is Corey Yellow Boy, who works with the Oglala Lakota County School District 65-1 as the Lakota Cultural Resources Director, where he supports Lakota Language teachers and develops cultural curriculum. Corey is an enrolled member of the Oglala Sioux Tribe, and he resides in the Calico community on the Pine Ridge Reservation in South Dakota. He holds a BA in Lakota Studies and an MA in Lakota Leadership and Management, both from Oglala Lakota College. For over a decade, Corey taught Lakota culture, language, history, and traditional art at the college. Corey's contributions to the series include consultation, advocacy, assistance in acquisitions, and our blind peer review process.

Suzzanne is a long-time teacher, historian, and publisher. She is a *summa cum laude* graduate of the University of Texas at Austin, an award-winning teacher and scholar, and—since her hire in 2015—the first woman publisher in the seventy-five-year history of NDSU Press. In her publishing career, Suzzanne has shepherded more than one hundred books through production, many of them from emerging authors that have gone on to win state, regional, and national awards.

The vision behind CVIP is to feature the authentic stories, poetry, and scholarly works of Native Americans, First Nations, Maori, Aboriginal Australians, Indians, and more to give voice to contemporary Indigenous peoples. Authors are asked to affirm their Indigenous identity and cultural connections. North Dakota State University Press adheres to a solemn commitment to avoid the damaging impact of cultural appropriation.

Published in the series:

- Volume 1 *Apple in the Middle*, middle grade novel by Dawn Quigley, 2018
- Volume 2 *Stringing Rosaries: The History, the Unforgivable, and the Healing of Northern Plains American Indian Boarding School Survivors*, nonfiction by Denise K. Lajimodiere, 2019
- Volume 3 *His Feathers Were Chains*, poetry by Denise K. Lajimodiere, 2020
- Volume 4 *The Shining Hands of My Ponca Ancestors*, a memoir in essays by Cliff Taylor, 2025

What people are saying about *The Shining Hands of My Ponca Ancestors*:

The Shining Hands of My Ponca Ancestors reveals tales of commonplace miracles using beloved and shared gestures and vernaculars—inside jokes to Turtle Island peoples. Cliff Taylor brings hope for the future to readers of all clans, speaking in the voice of a cousin-brother, casually poetic with each story, as our relatives do: strengthening our relationships to prayer, song, dance, feast and land, weaving promises for coming generations who will need them. His stories fall warm, honest, welcoming, the reclamation of his nation-heart, kind yet fierce, alive with memory. Gritty in moments, emotionally suspenseful, accountable to tradition, energizing us with familiar intimacy of friendly narrative, *Shining Hands* is a cradleboard of ancestral loving care.

—Pixie Lighthorse, *The Wound Makes the Medicine*

Cliff Taylor's *The Shining Hands of My Ponca Ancestors* is a poetic memoir and storytelling odyssey of personal and communal restoration. Cliff's experiences growing up as an urban Native in Columbus, Nebraska, and reconnecting to Northern Ponca ceremony and culture are told through a series of engaging vignettes. The stories in this collection are teeming with healing love and serve as a medicinal roadmap for other Native peoples to follow in proudly finding and reclaiming their Native cultures and kinship bonds.

Another powerful theme throughout Cliff's narrative is how his individual journey of healing and engagement with Native traditions follows the trajectory of the Northern Ponca's own cultural renaissance. The Ponca's long journey toward regaining federal recognition in 1990 came about after enduring many hardships and heartbreaks—not unlike Cliff's own circumstances and many other individual Ponca. There is beauty in witnessing Cliff's own healing and reconnection to ceremony and tradition occurring alongside the Northern Ponca's restoration. Cliff's work reminds us that just as there is intergenerational trauma in Native communities, there is also intergenerational healing.

—Brady DeSanti, Co-Editor of *Understanding and Teaching Native American History*

Luminous, honest, moving, and warm, Cliff Taylor's *The Shining Hands of My Ponca Ancestors* is offered in a voice as sublimely natural, poetic, and unflinchingly real as any you'll ever encounter. This book is a shining gift.

—Joy Castro, *The Truth Book and Island of Bones*

Ponca poet Cliff Taylor's new collection of essays is also the stuff of poetry and dreams—a delightful series of narrative effusions on Indigenous identity and ancestral voices, on his Ponca homeland in Nebraska, on Ponca traditions and folklore, all revelatory of Taylor's own visionary verve and zany zest for life. And if you ever wanted to know how Cliff came to believe in the little people, this is the book for you!

—Thomas C. Gannon, *Birding While Indian: A Mixed-Blood Memoir*